CROSS THE LINES

A Journey to Complete
The Marathon Grand Slam

William Thomas

DL

Published by DL Press
A division of Designing Leaders, LLC

Copyright © 2016 by William Thomas

All Rights Reserved. Passages from this book may be reproduced for research and reporting purposes, so long as proper attribution is provided. Contact the publisher for information regarding reprinting or the use of extended portions of this book.

Published in the United States by DL Press,
a division of Designing Leaders, LLC.

www.designingleaders.com

ISBN: 978-0-9982168-0-5

Dedicated to Pheidippides,
who in 490 B.C. ran from Marathon to Athens
to tell the Athenians of a victory in battle,
before immediately dropping dead.

All marathoners remember
that the first person who did this
died.

Author's Note

Even an individual long-distance runner is never alone.

Throughout this book I talk about different people, but I often keep their names to myself because, when we were doing whatever we were doing, they had no idea I might be writing about them someday. For that matter, neither did I. In any case, since most of them had no prior warning, I do not always attribute actions and words to the individuals involved. That being said, there is no way I would be where I am now without a lot of support along the way. There are many important people in my life, and some have been instrumental in this particular journey.

One name that shows up here a lot is Ethan Ngo. We met in 2006 when I arrived in Washington DC, and he was the person who first suggested I run a marathon. In the years since then we have had the chance to run races together in the US, France, Thailand, and Australia. As I pursued my Grand Slam goal, he decided that he wanted to complete the 7 Continents, and as of this writing in 2016 he has completed six, with only Antarctica remaining. Whether he will go for the North Pole, and finish the Grand Slam himself, is anyone's guess, but I hope he does. He was the first one to believe in me, even before I believed in myself.

I met my best friend, Linh Le, when he arrived in Washington DC for graduate school. A native of Vietnam, he initially sought me out because I was working in international relations, the field that he was studying. He was helpful in the early days of running, occasionally letting me crash on his couch when his apartment was a lot closer to the Starting Line than mine was, and he sets an example of both intellectual curiosity and personal fitness that I try to emulate. It was Linh who was with me on my birthday in 2010 when I decided to pursue the Grand Slam; he was the first person I told, and he has been a source of support every day since then. After a race, Ethan and Linh are the first people I contact, and they are the last people I would want to disappoint.

Other friends, whether runners or not, have kept me going along this journey. Zuoren Pan would watch for me near the Finish Line at races in Singapore, even at 4:30am when I finished an overnight marathon. He was also the first person to suggest writing this book. Stan Yau was very supportive, and patient, during my first year of running, always making sure that the big cinnamon rolls that were my motivation were waiting after I finished a long Saturday morning training run. When I was assigned to the Pentagon, Ambassador Charles Ray and Colonel Dave Ellis ensured that my peers and I took time during the day to maintain our fitness, and they also supported my Fulbright Scholar experience that allowed me to run on my second continent. Some of my college friends, especially David Price and Greg Ashe, kept up the support from far away over the years. Azhan Rabi made me happy by telling me I was the inspiration for running his own first marathon, and made me happier by flying to Singapore from Malaysia so we could run a race together.

Moving from culture to culture as I lived in new countries over the years could be a little stressful, which always had the potential to disrupt my running. My transition into Asia was made a lot smoother by some great friends, including William Ng, Derek Lee, Edmund Chan, Greg Leon, Ryan de Sotto, and Ace Le. Whenever I felt like a fish out of water, they were always able to make me feel comfortable again.

My years in Singapore were greatly enhanced by the New Balance Runners, the first running group I ever joined. They not only helped me to be a better runner, they also helped give me a stronger sense of community. Eugene Tan always seemed to get my best performance out of me, and if I could run a race with him I think I could easily set a new personal best. Terence Beh, Kenneth Chan, Andrew Lin Yikai, and Ashley Yong all helped make those Thursday evening runs pretty special. A big thanks goes to Edmund Lim, who leads the runs and has provided great advice for me over the years.

There are two elite Singaporean runners who have had a very positive influence on me. Soh Rui Yong and Ashley Liew both ran for Singapore in the 2015 Southeast Asian Games, with Rui Yong winning the gold. I got a chance to run with them and other elites a week before the Games, and since then they have stayed in touch and supported me in various races even as they have pursued their own goals. One of the things I like about this sport is that amateurs can run with the best in the world, and those at the top still see those amateurs as part of their peer group.

Near the end of my Grand Slam journey I received critical support from two companies who also gave me the chance to share my stories with a wider audience. In exchange for interviews and articles about my adventures, the marketing team and my local branch's leadership at Virgin Active Thailand provided me with a gym membership, while Matt Fox and his folks at Flight Centre Active Travel Singapore helped to sponsor my air travel.

A big thank you has to go to Richard Donovan, who created the North Pole Marathon in 2002, which then led to the idea of the Marathon Grand Slam. As race director for the North Pole and the Antarctic Ice Marathon, as well as other adventure races such as the Volcano Marathon and the World Marathon Challenge, Richard has created the opportunity for runners to not only see the world but also see what they are capable of achieving. Without him, I never would have had this goal to strive for in the first place.

Finally, the rest of my family has set examples that I have finally followed. My father Ray started running marathons around the same age that I did, and was still running shorter distances into his 70s, before deciding that long walks might be the better option. My mother Rosemary has been going to the gym regularly for many years, since long before I was. My younger brother Chuck has been working out for many years, and his muscular bulk leads people to be surprised when I refer to him as my "little brother." I was the only one in the family who was not paying attention to my fitness, though I would like to think I have fixed that now.

~ 1 ~
The Starting Line

I run marathons because I am lazy.

As contradictory as that might sound, it is the truth. I realize, though, that it might need a little explanation.

In the autumn of 2007 I had just returned from a very short military deployment to Afghanistan, where I was helping set up the faculty for their National Military Academy. While there, the only things to do were work and work out, so I came back after two months in better shape than I had been in for a while. I wanted to keep that, and I knew I should be running for my health, and generally taking better care of myself.

I also knew that I get bored easily, and if history were a guide, I would start running but then give up after a while. I had similarly returned from Iraq in 2005 in pretty good shape, and I reverted to my previous fitness levels within six months. I had not run farther than 5K since college, and the odds that I would start running and keep it up almost 20 years after graduation were slim.

About that same time, Ethan, one of my closest friends, ran the Marine Corps Marathon in Washington DC. I was very impressed by what he had done, especially since he had only started running within the last year and now had already run a marathon. As I talked with him, he said, "Why don't you sign up for next year's Marine Corps Marathon, and tell everyone you are going to do it, so you won't quit." It is amazing how one sentence from a friend can lead you to reinvent your life.

I began running at age 42, with my first marathon coming about nine months after I first put on a pair of running shoes. When I told people what I was planning to do, I got a lot of skepticism in return. It was brushed off as a New Year's resolution that would soon fade into memory. I was told that I was nowhere near the shape in which I needed to be to do something like that. Some said I should set my sights lower, maybe aiming for a 10K race. I heard a wide range of opinions, but a lot of them came down to one key point: you are too old to be starting this.

In the months that followed, I proved the naysayers wrong. I ran that first marathon in October 2008. Six weeks later, I ran my second one. Nine weeks after that, I ran my third. I do not recommend running three marathons within 15 weeks – and I do not have any plans to do that again – but it showed me that my age was not going to be a barrier.

As my 44th birthday approached in January 2010, I started looking for a new goal, and stumbled across some races that would lead to an interesting objective. So, with four marathons under my belt, I set a new goal: I would run the Marathon Grand Slam by the time I turned 50. The Grand Slam consists of running a marathon on all seven continents and at the North Pole, a feat very few people had accomplished. Again, there was skepticism. Again, there were questions about why I was wasting my time. Again, there was the implicit notion that I was too old to be doing something like this. And again, I proved them wrong.

On April 16, 2016, I crossed the Finish Line of the North Pole Marathon, about 50 kilometers from the geographic North Pole. I was three months past my 50th birthday, and I was not the oldest runner among the small group of finishers. At the conclusion of that race there were only 82 people in the world who had fully completed the Marathon Grand Slam, and I was one of them.

Throughout the years between the time I started running and the time I finished the Grand Slam, I learned so many lessons. I learned about fitness and nutrition, I learned about my abilities and my potential, I learned about self-discipline and persistence. The most important lesson I learned, though, is that it is never too late to chase a dream.

So many people told me I was wasting my time, so many people said I was too old, and if I had listened to them I would not have had the adventures and achievements I have had during the last few years. I also would not be looking forward to the many adventures that are still to come. A lot of things in life can stand in your way of achieving something, but your age and your own attitude should not be among them.

As I shared running stories from around the world with my friends, one suggestion that kept coming up was that I should be writing these down. Sure, there were Facebook posts and blog entries and my own journals that captured some of the tales, but the lessons I learned only seemed to emerge in conversations. I finally decided that there might be something here worth sharing, and the idea for this book was born.

When I started writing the stories of the individual races on each continent and at the North Pole, I realized there was a lot more to the story than simply what happened on race day. Throughout this period I have been a military officer, university professor, international consultant, and small business owner. My homes have included Washington DC, Singapore, and Bangkok. I have trained alone, with a friend, and in a running club. So much has happened during these past few years, and now I see that all of it is connected. Even if I could not be sure of how I would reach my ultimate destination, the personal and professional decisions I made along the way all led me to the place I was aiming for.

Throughout the book some of the terminology may not always seem consistent, and that is simply a reflection of the global nature of my experiences. I'm an American, so I typically think in terms of "miles," but since most of my marathons have been in other countries, I will talk about "kilometers" as well. I may write about Sydney Harbour, because that is how the Australians spell it, but in my mind I was running toward "the harbor" because I learned in school that an extra "u" is too fancy for Americans. The changing nature of the writing mirrors the changing nature of my life during the years of this journey.

I like to think this book will offer different things to different people. Some may draw lessons from it that help in their personal life, others may see things they can bring to a leadership role at work. For some this will inspire them to run, for others it will make them want to travel more. However a reader sees this book, I hope they take away the most important point: it is never too late to chase your dreams and try something new, so rather than regretting something that you did not try, just get out there and try it.

~

I was not even remotely athletic as a kid. Skinny, bookish, uncoordinated, and pretty much uninterested in being any kind of athlete, I was the stereotypical "last kid picked for the team" just about every time. Long before kickball became an ironic game played by hipsters in major American cities, it was the only elementary school "sport" at which I ever felt competent.

That is not to say I never tried. I played in a youth basketball league for two years, and scored a grand total of two points in my second year, which was much better than the zero points my first year. In high school I gave the tennis team a shot, and found myself quickly relegated to the junior varsity "B" squad, which consisted of the kids who wanted to be on the team but who had no talent. Coaches in all cases pretty much ignored me, either having no interest in me or seeing that I was not all that interested myself.

My successes tended to come in the classroom, and that probably encouraged my individualistic streak. Growing up in the 1970s and 80s, education was very much individually-focused, without the group work and emphasis on collaborative skills that are more common today. My success on my own made me feel okay that I was not part of a team.

I still had group activities, of course, being in the Cub Scouts and Boy Scouts, so it's not like I did everything on my own. At age 13, though, I was already an Eagle Scout, so I didn't feel the pull to stay in the organization. I always seem to be looking for the next achievement, and I felt like I had run out of them there.

It was the Boy Scouts that, in a roundabout way, sealed my image as a non-athlete. During a physical exam before summer camp, the doctor noticed something wrong with my spine. In addition to a mild S-curvature, known as scoliosis, he also detected a forward curvature, called kyphosis or, more officially, Scheuermann's Disease. When you see someone described as a "hunchback" – a name I heard often over the next few years – there is a good chance they are suffering from kyphosis.

My mom's younger brother had a similar condition, and it led to health problems when a lot of his organs were compressed against his rib cage as his upper body bent forward. Determined to avoid the same fate for me, we started treatment, which for teenagers consisted of two options: surgically implanting rods in the back to hold it straight, or wearing a back brace for a few years to hold the spine straight while I continued to grow. We went with the brace, a device I have seen depicted in a number of comedy films because, after all, it's fun to laugh at a kid in a back brace, right?

Just in case you think teenagers are kind to their peers who are different, let me correct you: they are not. The years from age 14 to 16 were not at all fun for me. In addition to general ridicule from other kids, I felt like I was held back from a lot of different activities that everyone else was enjoying. Though some good friends stuck by me, this experience further reinforced my individualistic nature, and left me even less interested in sports.

One element of my life that really shaped me was that my dad was in the Air Force, and so we moved someplace new about every three years. I grew up in places as different as Florida, Virginia, Nebraska, California, and North Dakota. This exposed me to a lot of different cultures, and it also gave me a chance to "start over" in a new place. About the same time I ended the brace therapy, after my sophomore year in high school, we moved to Nebraska. That gave me two years to rebuild my confidence in a new place before heading off to college.

My dad had started running a few years earlier, while we were living in southern California, and that really picked up when we moved to Nebraska. He was running marathons by this point, ultimately doing well enough to qualify for the Boston Marathon but, due to the demands of his military life, he was never able to get the time off to actually go run it. You might think that with a runner in the family I would have picked it up too, but the years with the back brace pretty much killed any athletic interest I might have had.

When I went to register for classes at Bellevue West High School in Nebraska, I found that I still had to take one more year of physical education. My experiences in PE class during the previous couple of years at Minot High School in North Dakota had been pretty negative, so I had been looking forward to not having to take that class anymore.

There was, however, another option. Instead of PE, I could enroll in Air Force Junior ROTC, a high school version of the military officer training program available at many universities. I had already decided I did not want to go into the Air Force like my dad, probably out of a typical teenaged attitude of wanting to do the exact opposite of your parents. Once I joined JROTC, though, I realized I was actually pretty good at this, so perhaps trying for an Air Force scholarship to pay for university and going into the military afterwards was not a bad idea. As it turned out, my avoidance of physical activity put me onto a long-term career path that still defines my life in many ways.

~

For many years, when someone asked me where I was from, I would answer "Virginia." The reality is that I never felt like I was "from" anywhere, since we moved around so much. However, my four years at the University of Virginia – which, at that point, was the longest time I had spent in any one place – were the years in which I felt like I grew up. UVA is, in many ways, my hometown.

Nearly 30 years after I graduated, the University (and yes, that is always capitalized) remains a cornerstone of my life. Founded in 1819 by Thomas Jefferson, who had written the Declaration of Independence and served as the third President of the United States, UVA remains one of the top-ranked universities in the US. The students come from all over, the faculty is amazing, and the Grounds have been named a UNESCO World Heritage site. For an 18-year old from Nebraska, it was a new world.

This was my first time away from home, and it opened my eyes to what was possible. My parents were wonderful, but they were also a little bit overprotective at times. The years in the back brace may have contributed to that, but whatever the reason, UVA offered a chance to spread my wings and fly…literally.

During my first semester, some friends decided we should try skydiving. I told my mom, only to have her say, "Oh, I would be so scared for you, please don't do that!" I didn't, but only because the weather was bad that day and we cancelled it. When we rescheduled it two weeks later, I simply didn't tell her. Arriving home at Christmas, I showed each of my parents a photo of me hanging under a parachute, drifting down. Dad said, "Don't tell your mom," and Mom said, "Don't tell your dad." It was quite a while before both realized the other already knew about it.

Our first year dorm consisted of suites with 5 double rooms, so ten of us – collectively known as The Aristocrat Club – had a chance to develop some great friendships early on. Many of us continued to live with each other during our four years, and even before Facebook we managed to stay connected in the years following graduation.

I used my time at the University to explore a lot of interests. With my Air Force scholarship I already knew I had a job waiting for me after graduation, so I decided to take classes that would be interesting and challenging, without worrying about the negative impact that might have on my grades. I studied Russian to fulfill my foreign language requirement, I took fast-paced calculus courses, and while I certainly felt like I learned a lot, my grades never reflected that.

It was tough to go from being one of the top students in my high school, to being surrounded by people who were all among the top students in their high school. At a place like the University, some people are going to end up with grades they have never seen before. That was a shock to my system, but it also forced me to reevaluate my priorities and figure out what I really wanted to get out of my four years.

As a result, a lot of what I learned came from activities outside the classroom. I had been in school bands ever since elementary school, so I stayed active in the Pep Band and later in the Symphonic Band. My Air Force ROTC activities took up a lot of time, and I ended up serving as the Corps Commander during the fall semester of my last year. One thing I didn't really do much of, though, was sports.

Despite being in military training and having to meet certain physical requirements, I never got involved in intramural sports or even individual fitness. During my first year I played in one tennis tournament and got beaten so badly in the first round that I never tried again. I did some running with an ROTC colleague during my second year, but other than that I pretty much did only what was required. The one exception was a short race I ran with my roommate Dave, an event we still refer to as "the Fetus 5K" because it was a benefit for a newborn care unit at a hospital and the image on the t-shirt was, well, a fetus.

~

After graduating in May 1988 with a degree in economics and being commissioned as a second lieutenant in the Air Force, I spent a few months working for a company in Washington DC until it was time to report to my first assignment. My friend Stan and I were being assigned as intercontinental ballistic missile launch officers in Wyoming. Typically known as "missileers," we first had to report to Vandenberg Air Force Base in southern California for training before we could adopt that title.

There is a common perception of the military, driven largely by Hollywood, that we all get up before dawn and can be seen running in groups across the base. That is true in some environments, but not in most places, and certainly not at ICBM launch officer training. Our work was done in classrooms and simulators, and we spent a lot of time studying in our dorms and in the classified vaults at the training center. Few of us worried about going to the gym or running. We were more concerned about studying. We had seen what happened to people who failed the program; the training squadron's administrative officer was someone who had flunked out, and none of us wanted to be his replacement.

Stan and I graduated and moved on to the 400th Strategic Missile Squadron at F.E. Warren Air Force Base in Cheyenne, Wyoming in August 1989. Ronald Reagan had only recently left the White House, the Soviet Union was still "the evil empire," we were in the Strategic Air Command, and the Cold War was going strong. The 400th was the only squadron operating the Peacekeeper ICBM, the newest and most powerful missile in the US arsenal, and as the system was further developed, the junior officers expected to be in the initial cadre of the next version within a few years. Those plans lasted for only a couple of months.

As a missileer, my primary job involved going "on alert" about 8 times a month, which consisted of a 24-hour shift with my crew partner in a launch control center about 60 feet underground, monitoring and maintaining ten ICBMs. During an otherwise normal alert in November, we watched on our small TV as the Berlin Wall came down and the Cold War began to end. It was an interesting night, since we were not sure if peace was breaking out, or if Soviet tanks would start rumbling through the holes in the wall and into West Berlin.

During the next two years I saw plenty of world events unfold while I sat in that little underground room. I watched a coup in Moscow, when no one really knew where their nuclear codes were. I followed Operations DESERT SHIELD and DESERT STORM as the world fought its first war against Saddam Hussein's Iraq. I listened to Mikhail Gorbachev's speech in which he dismantled the Soviet Union. Through it all, as the threat of global nuclear war and the end of humanity thankfully receded, one little thought stayed at the back of my mind: world peace is great, but hey, there goes my career.

Despite the changes in the world that were affecting the ICBM mission, I still had some interesting opportunities during the four years I was stationed in Wyoming. A couple of those years were spent as an instructor, which gave me my first sense of teaching, something I really enjoyed. I went back to Vandenberg for six weeks as part of a program to launch an unarmed Peacekeeper missile at a test range in the Pacific. It was an interesting feeling to actually turn the key and have it lift off, something I had spent years training for but hoped never to have to do in the real world. Through all of this, though, I knew I needed to figure out what I wanted to do next, because my plans for a career in ICBMs had crumbled along with the Berlin Wall.

I briefly considered going into a program to become an Air Force lawyer. Though I got into a couple of law schools, I was not accepted into the Air Force's legal education program, so that door closed. I had spent much of my free time earning an MBA at Regis University in Denver, and I looked at the possibility of leaving the military and using my degree in the private sector. One of the lieutenants working for me, though, was an Air Force Academy graduate, and he suggested I look into teaching there, since only a master's degree was required for entry-level instructors. I applied for a position, was quickly interviewed and accepted, and soon moved to Colorado Springs, Colorado.

The Academy combines a four-year college with rigorous military training; the graduates leave as Air Force officers with a bachelor's degree. Teaching there was an excellent choice, not only because I got to work with some amazing people and get to know some fantastic students, but also because after my first semester I realized that teaching was what I really wanted to do. I spent four years on the faculty there, and knew I wanted to pursue this career path further.

One of the great opportunities the Academy offers is the chance to earn a PhD and then return to the faculty. The idea is to have a mix of faculty members: military officers with recent operational experience and a master's degree, civilian professors with a PhD, and a small number of military officers who combine their experience with a doctorate. I was selected to be part of that last group, and though there were a few bumps in the road as I got there – nothing in the military is ever easy – I checked in at George Mason University near Washington DC in 1999 to pursue my PhD in the School of Public Policy.

Going for my PhD was nothing like my earlier degrees. It was far more intense, but also more individualistic than my bachelor's and master's degree programs. Since every doctoral candidate identifies their own specialty, we tend to work on our own once we get away from the introductory classes. Most of my friends in Washington were not students but instead were pursuing normal careers, and so they may not have always understood what I was doing. They soon learned not to ask about my research, because I could easily go off on a two-hour monologue explaining the most fascinating things I had learned that week.

I had come to my program with a specific research question: why did the Air Force have so much trouble adapting to the post-Cold War world? Both at the Academy and in a follow-on assignment, I had seen senior officers who were still thinking only in terms of global war. As a result, many young officers were leaving the military because they felt they were not getting the resources, training, or support they needed for the missions they were actually doing, such as peacekeeping and nation-building. The 1990s had been a difficult transition period for the military, especially for the Air Force, and I wanted to understand why.

The funding program that sent me to school would only last for three years, so I needed to complete my degree in that time. My friend Jim, who would end up being my boss when I returned to the Academy, suggested that every paper I wrote for a class should somehow address my research question, so all the work I did during my first two years could be used for my dissertation. This was the best advice I could have gotten, and following it was the only way I could complete my degree on time. As it turned out, I actually had to register for an additional semester after I left, so I could be officially enrolled when it came time for my dissertation defense. Finally, though, I walked across the stage at graduation, and when I returned to my seat and heard an undergraduate behind me say, "Congratulations, Doctor," I knew I was on a great new path for the rest of my life.

I ended up having to do a one-year assignment after grad school, but following that I finally got back to the Academy. This time around I was the deputy director of a research institute and was also teaching both military strategy and political science. By the time I returned, the US and other countries had already invaded both Afghanistan and Iraq. I felt confident about the mission in Afghanistan, because that was where the 9/11 plot was hatched, and it was important to find the people responsible and also remove that country as a safe haven for the bad guys. I was not, however, comfortable with the invasion of Iraq. I could see no good reason for it, and it took resources away from a more necessary mission in Afghanistan.

It is not in my nature to criticize things I know nothing about, nor do I like to sit on the sidelines when there is something I can contribute. I was also thinking that, if my students were going to find themselves in these environments after graduation, it would be good if I had experience there too. One friend was already planning to go to Afghanistan to help develop the military there, so I started making inquiries into a similar role in Iraq, and soon enough found myself on a plane headed to the desert.

My deployment to Iraq only lasted four months – the Academy wanted me back during the spring semester – but that short time was an eye-opening experience. One thing I learned is that I really, really do not enjoy being shot at. I was also surprised by the lack of preparation that many people, including me, had for that situation. That improved in the years that followed, based in part on the experiences we had, but in 2004-2005 many people were figuring things out as they went along.

As I settled into a routine there, one way to break up the boredom was to hit the gym that had been put into place in an old storage building. Back home I would have had plenty of other distractions, but other than working and eating there was not much else to do here, so it was the gym or nothing. Most of my time was spent either on a stationary bike or lifting weights.

Though I was a military officer, I was never the big, bulky soldier you see in the movies. In fact, I really was not fit at all. At various times I had tried to start running or going to the gym, but the odd work schedule I had made it impossible to be consistent, and that gave me an easy excuse to stop. The Air Force's physical fitness requirements were pretty limited at that point: we had to complete a 1.5-mile run in a certain period, and I could always manage to do that once a year. I told friends, "As long as I can outrun the bad guys for a mile and a half without throwing up, I'm doing ok." The Iraq experience offered an opportunity to change.

Change I did, but only for a little while. Upon returning home I found I had lost weight around the middle while bulking up slightly in the chest. For the first time in many years I took the opportunity to buy new clothes in new sizes, and was determined to keep it up. That lasted a total of about six months, by which time any hope for regular exercise had faded, and I was back to my previous body shape.

When my Academy assignment ended I transferred to a role at the Pentagon, for two reasons. First, this particular organization – it was responsible for recovering and identifying the remains of POW and MIA military personnel overseas – was one I had always thought about joining, and an opportunity came up at the right moment. At the same time, I was a lieutenant colonel and had begun thinking that this next assignment would be my last, and I wanted to position myself in Washington DC, where I figured I would work after retiring from the Air Force.

The job was not quite what I expected – I spent more time rewriting Pentagon policy than I did negotiating with foreign governments – so when my former department head from the Academy told me he was going to Afghanistan, I asked if he could use an extra pair of hands. It turned out that he did need some help, and my bosses were okay with me going, so off I went to Afghanistan.

Kabul was a better experience for me than Baghdad had been. Not only did I not get shot at, I found Afghanistan's military officers to be much more motivated about learning what they needed to learn to take back control of their country. I was only there for two months, but when I left I had the feeling I had accomplished more there than I had in twice the time in Iraq.

Like Iraq, though, it was a case of "work and workout," because there was really nothing else to do. Returning home in good shape again, I was determined not to lose it this time. After discussing it with Ethan, and hearing his suggestion of running the following year's Marine Corps Marathon, I decided it was time to move toward that Starting Line.

~ 2 ~
26.2 Lessons From Running Marathons

I think I have learned more about life in the eight years since I started running than in the 42 years before that.

This book might fall into different categories – sports, travel, biography – but one thing it definitely is not is a murder mystery. So, there is no need to wait until the end to give away the secrets. Instead, I want to offer the lessons that emerged from my running experiences right up front, so it is easier to see how they developed as I went along this journey, and a reader can be thinking about how they may apply to his or her life.

As I started on the book I planned to include ten lessons, because that is a nice round number everyone is used to when making a list. Talking with friends, though, I realized there were more than ten worth sharing. Finally, someone suggested just making it 26 lessons, and I added one last thought at the end to provide the 0.2.

1. It Is Never Too Late to Start Something New

Age 42 might be the point where some marathoners decide they have had enough and hang it up, but for me, it was the time that I began. Plenty of people questioned whether it was too late for me to start something like this, but I found it best to ignore them. Once I saw the benefits of running I wished I had started earlier, but that regret was no reason not to make it happen now.

People who want to tear you down, or who are concerned when they don't need to be, will often say, "But you're too old!" Don't listen to those people. Everybody – and every body – is different. If something will be physically challenging or represents a huge shift in your life, your decision should be determined not by the date on your birth certificate but instead by the abilities and limitations of your body and mind. If you think you cannot have an exciting new adventure simply because of your age, you are sure to miss out on something great.

2. A Goal is Necessary, But Accountability Makes it Happen

When Ethan suggested I register for a marathon to stay motivated about running, he added one more step: tell everyone about it. His point was that if I told people about it I would be less likely to quit. No one wants to look bad in front of friends and family, so by making your goals public you have a stronger incentive to achieve them. When I look back at my Facebook timeline on April 30, 2008, I see it right there: "Will Thomas signed up today for a marathon in October." Would I have still done it without that? Maybe, but the chances were a lot greater once I put it out there.

I did something similar for the Grand Slam, though I was not quite as public about it at first. Once I shared my plans with Linh on my birthday I felt committed, but I did not tell other people yet. I thought it sounded a little cocky, with only four marathons under my belt, so I first wanted a better idea of how I would accomplish it. Over time, as I ran on various continents, I would mention that the race was part of a bigger plan, and my friends caught on and were watching for what would come next. I realized I should not make myself accountable until I first thought about how I was going to make my goals happen. Accountability helps keep you on track, but you should have an idea about what you are doing, and why, before you announce it to the rest of the world.

3. Nothing Happens in Isolation

As I started working on this book I initially was just writing a chapter about each race. Then I realized I needed to spell out some context, since the story behind the races was changing as I moved around the world. Once I started seeing the relationships between my professional decisions, my geographic choices, and my running goals, it hit me that all of these were connected. Every decision needed to take into consideration every other decision.

When you set a goal, it is important to understand the context in which you will pursue it. If you are unemployed, maybe focus on that before signing up for the North Pole Marathon. If you have a spouse or kids, talk with them about what you want to do rather than making a decision on your own. If it is a long-term goal, think about how your life might change and what that will do to your goal, or about how your goal might influence other decisions you need to make in the years to come. If something is important enough, it will affect, and be affected by, other important things in your life.

4. Be Both Optimistic and Realistic

I will never run in the Olympics, and I am okay with that. I will also never run a sub-2 hour marathon – it is possible that no one ever will – and that fact does not keep me awake at night. I told friends after the Antarctic Ice Marathon that, when the Race Director put the medal around my neck, that was my Olympic medal. I do not aim to do what others do as much as I try to achieve what I think is right for me.

There are things we can do today, things we have the potential to do in the future if we build up to it, and things we will never do. Do not spend your time worrying about that last category, but instead, focus your attention on the first and especially on the second. Take pleasure in the things you can do today, and get excited about the things you have the potential to do in the future. Set goals that are challenging but realistically possible; just make sure you define "realistically" pretty broadly in order to keep things interesting.

5. Your Priorities May Not Always Be Obvious

Once the journey toward the Grand Slam started, I needed to decide which races I should run. The most obvious idea was that I should only do races that contributed to the eight races I needed to do, but that was unrealistic. Just because they seemed like the top priority did not mean they were the only things I needed to consider. The travel alone was going to be expensive, plus there was the challenge of timing my races so I could do the ones I wanted. I preferred to have at least three months between them, and some of them were only a couple weeks apart on different continents. I created a plan for completing the Grand Slam over a few years, a plan that accounted for all the constraints, and that also included plenty of non-Grand Slam races just for fun and to make sure I kept up my training. There were steps that would help me achieve my goal, there were limitations to be overcome, and all of those had to be kept in balance if I was going to finish the Grand Slam.

When I was in Iraq, I once asked the head of our planning division about our priorities, and he replied. "As long as we have enough money, everything can be our number one priority." Of course, if everything is number one, then nothing really is. At some point you need to figure out what it will take to reach your goal, and prioritize among the many things you need to do so you can use your resources wisely. No matter how much money you have, no matter how much flexibility you think you have, there will always be at least one constraint: time. Everybody gets exactly 24 hours in a day, and how you choose to use those hours determines how successful you will be. Prioritizing among those things that are essential, that are important, and that are simply nice to have, will help you use your resources in a way that moves you toward your goal.

6. Do Not Underestimate the Power of an Audience

The first time I ran a 10-miler, the cheering crowds offered a real change from the quiet of a Saturday morning training run. One of the smartest things I did in later races was to make sure my name was on my shirt, because hearing people yelling your name when you run down the street is fantastic. Nobody likes to look bad in front of a crowd, so the race spectators offer a great boost to falling energy levels. That became even more obvious when I started running outside the US, where spectators are not as common. The silence is almost eerie. If accountability makes a plan more likely to come together, then a supportive audience certainly makes it more fun.

No matter what you are doing, if you prepare for something by yourself, it is going to feel very different in front of others. Whether it's giving a presentation in front of 500 people or perfecting your sales pitch for a single client, it feels different once you are in front of someone else. Take that as a positive difference, and find a way to make use of it. If you can, consider preparing with friends or colleagues watching you, to better simulate what the real environment will be like. Many people get nervous in front of others, but their impact can be very positive if you let it.

7. You Are Stronger Than You Think

In 2016 some interesting research was published about marathoners' memories of a race a week later. By collecting runners' perceptions of pain and fatigue during a race, and then asking them about their recollections a week later, researchers found that runners generally did not remember it being as bad as it seemed at the time. Perhaps your brain is playing tricks on you, making you think you are more tired than you really are. From my own experience I know there have been plenty of times when it felt like my body just did not want to go any faster, but then in the last couple of kilometers my pace gets dramatically faster, suggesting I had quite a bit of energy left all along.

When you are trying to do something challenging, your most important body part is your brain. If you tell yourself you can do it, then you have a chance. If you tell yourself that you cannot, you will most likely prove yourself to be correct. No matter what the challenge may be, knowing that you are likely to remember it as being less difficult than it seems now can help. Try to bring that feeling forward from the future and use it now, telling yourself that what you are doing is not as difficult as you are making it out to be. Bringing a positive attitude does not guarantee success, of course, but it can open up pockets of strength that you did not realize you had.

8. Listen to Your Body

The preceding thoughts notwithstanding, if you are feeling more than mental fatigue, and instead are getting specific warnings from your body, you need to pay attention. Traveling to marathons around the world has exposed me to plenty of weather conditions and the physical effects they can cause. Whether it is dizziness and dehydration in Singapore's heat or the numbness in the toes that can signal frostbite at the North Pole, your body has ways of letting you know when something is not going right. Many runners will push through and decide to deal with it after the finish, but biology is not always so forgiving.

Your body has warning signs for a reason. When you feel pain, when you feel dizzy, when you feel fatigued all the time rather than just when running long distances, that is your body's way of telling you that something is wrong and you need to address it. This is true when running a marathon, just as it is true when running a business, or when running around getting your kids to their activities. If you are overstressed and cannot focus, talk to someone. If you see physical symptoms that something is wrong, check with your doctor. Your body will tell you when you need to change what you are doing, and you really should pay attention to it. You may not get a second warning before something goes horribly wrong.

9. You Do Not Have To Change Everything

I know I should be getting up earlier and running in the mornings. I live in Southeast Asia, where even the night can be hot and humid; once the sun comes up, the temperature climbs pretty quickly. I have also seen the research showing that working out first thing in the morning helps with weight loss and energizes your mind for the rest of the day. All the signs suggest I should go to bed earlier and get up earlier, but that simply is not happening, and I am okay with that.

Despite what the evidence tells me, my body seems to have an energy cycle during the day that works for me. I get my best work done at certain times of the day, and the pre-dawn hours simply do not fit into that schedule. As much as I focus on self-improvement, I am not convinced that I need to force myself to change everything. No one should. If there are things in your life that feel natural, that seem to work for you, that do not conflict with any of your life's goals, and that carry a cost that you are willing to accept, then maybe those things do not need to change. In my work I see a lot of clients trying to change things in their business without understanding why they want to. I am convinced that "change for the sake of change" is a bad idea, so rather than trying to change everything in your life, focus instead on those things you really want to do differently, and keep on doing everything else. You can avoid a lot of stress that way.

10. You Will Fail

In the 2010 New York City Marathon, I beat one of the greatest distance runners in the world, Haile Gebrselassie, who at the time held the world record for the marathon. When I say, "I beat him," what I actually mean is that he had to drop out of the race at around 16 miles due to an injury, whereas I completed the race. That reinforced for me the idea that even the best in the world are not perfect, that there are times they will succeed and, yes, times that they will fail.

I believe there are two kinds of runners in the world: those who have DNF'd ("Did Not Finish") and those who will. When you are pushing your limits, there are no guarantees of success; that is what makes it exciting. Runners can control many things, such as their training schedule, their diet, their shoes and other running gear, and the races in which they plan to run, but there are plenty of things that can happen that get between a runner and the Finish Line. I see the same thing with my business clients; they often look for innovative ideas, but trying something new means sometimes they fail. There are no guarantees of success no matter how much experience we have or how much we prepare. If you never fail, you are not taking enough chances.

11. Running Solo Can Be Harder

Running often becomes an individual activity. Most of my running has been on my own; even with a training partner or a club, I might run with others only once or twice a week. Simply lacing up your shoes and getting out onto the trail whenever you have the opportunity, rather than worrying about coordinating with other peoples' schedules, means running can be very solitary. I found, though, that improving was harder when I ran by myself. Going back to the idea of accountability, having others around me pushes me to maintain a pace that I might not push myself to on my own. Running with people who are faster than I also tends to pull me along and get me to a speed that helps more in terms of both health and race preparation.

If you are trying to improve your skills in some area, you are more likely to do that with others around rather than completely on your own. No matter how high the standards you set for yourself, you might never push yourself as hard when you are alone as you will when you are with others. You need to consider your goals: if you are simply trying to relax, then doing something on your own can be perfect. When you are trying to improve, though, it can often be much harder to do that by yourself.

12. Surround Yourself With People Who Make You Better

As I pursued my goals, things got much more interesting when I surrounded myself with people who added something to my life. Ethan and Linh set fitness examples that I try to emulate, Linh and Stan help me understand international relations better, Zuoren improves my understanding of the blend between geopolitics and business, while

William in Malaysia and Ace in Singapore help me find new things about cultures and places that I did not know before.

If the ideas of lifelong learning and self-improvement are important for you, then surround yourself with people who make you better. We often choose to do this through the authors we read, the mentors we select at work, or the influencers we follow on LinkedIn, but it helps to bring that into your personal life. I made a decision years ago that if someone was determined to be negative and bring me down, that person has no place in my life. Rather than spending time with people mindlessly, I have chosen to surround myself with people who make me better – hoping, of course, that they want me around, too – and it has made a huge difference not only in specific knowledge or skills but also, more importantly, in creating a very positive outlook on life that helps me set new goals and achieve them.

13. Do Not Do Something New On Race Day

A couple of times, I have violated the cardinal rule of marathons: don't try anything for the first time on race day. That does not just apply to wearing new shoes, it means not even wearing new socks or a shirt. It absolutely means not drinking something new along the route; when asked for advice about traveling to overseas marathons, the first thing I tell people is to find out what isotonic drinks they are serving at the aid stations and make sure you try them before race day. You do not want to be out on the course and suddenly have a problem, because your opportunities to fix it are limited at that point.

When you prepare for something, you can set your mind at ease by creating some consistency and reducing uncertainty. The more that the actual event matches your preparation, the better off you will be. If you are giving a PowerPoint presentation, try it out on the computer you will be using with the projector that's going to be attached, just in case it looks different. If you have a big job interview, don't pick that day to see just how spicy of a taco you can handle. Be very careful about doing something new when you don't have a chance to fix a problem during the event, and when the cost of failure would be high.

14. If You Do Not Know Your Limits, It Is Hard to Exceed Them

When I go out for a training run I always carry my card for the local public transit system as well as money for a taxi, or for a bottle of water from a street vendor or convenience store. There have been days when I have pushed myself to my limit, whether in terms of distance, time, or weather, showing me just how far I can go. Then, once I know where that limit is, I can decide if I want to push beyond it, and figure out what I have to do to make that happen.

There is no shame in acknowledging that you cannot go any further. If you never know how far you can go today, you will never know what opportunities for growth are out there. The trick is to not set low expectations for yourself, nor to shy away from further challenges once you hit your limit, but instead, to see that limit as a starting point for your improvement. A Singapore runner going by the name Ah Siao (which essentially means "crazy one") planned to run his first marathon and, in a bid to gain awareness for Singapore's Bone Marrow Donor Programme, he would run it while dragging a large truck tire attached to him with a rope. In his first practice attempt he only got two kilometers before stopping, but instead of quitting, he used that to then build up to three, and then four, to the point that he ultimately went on to run and finish the race. He never knew what objectives he had to work toward until he knew what he was already capable of.

15. Aim High, But Also Recognize Your Accomplishments

My second continent was Asia, and I checked it off the list only six weeks after my first marathon. When I moved to Singapore to teach for a semester I took advantage of the opportunity to run a race there, but finished almost 20 minutes slower than my previous marathon. The heat had really gotten to me, and during the later miles I found myself walking for a while because I was starting to get dizzy. I wondered if my performance back in Washington DC had merely been a fluke.

Even though this was only my second marathon, I already had the mindset that I must get faster every time. That is not a complete surprise, of course; who among us does not want to improve? It occurred to me later, though, that I needed to recognize my achievements, and be happy about them. This is an ongoing struggle for me, and one of these days, I need to find a balance between working toward my own high standards while also acknowledging that what I have achieved is impressive compared to where I started. Sometimes, it is okay to get the A- rather than the A.

16. Move Forward, Or Get Out of the Way

Runners need to go at their own pace. Whether fast or slow, everyone has a speed that is right for them, based on their goals, their preparation, and other factors unique to each individual. Since many marathoners race "to complete, not compete," they should run at the pace they choose. That means slower runners should be able to run slowly, but they should also move out of the way of those who want to run faster. For that matter, people who decide to stop for selfies – or even text and make calls – really need to step aside. If that is what people choose to do, their right to focus on their technology does not give them the right to block others.

The same is true in other aspects of life, such as in the workplace. If you are comfortable in a role and have no desire to go further, then it is great you have found something you enjoy, but you may have people coming up behind you who still want to advance. If you do not find a way to help them get around you and continue on, if you end up being a roadblock on the corporate ladder, then someone else may decide how to move you out of the way, and you might not like the result. Similarly, in any relationship you have, whether professional or personal, you need to understand that your desires are not the only ones that matter. If you are going to be around other people, you need to take everyone's interests into account, not just your own.

17. Plan for Everything, Expect Nothing

Singapore marathoner Soh Rui Yong posted this phrase on Facebook as he prepared for the 2015 Fukuoka Marathon, and it captures an attitude you need to bring to race day. As you prepare for a race you may have a training schedule, proper nutrition, and shoes that are broken in just enough, but the universe does not always care about what you have done to get ready. On any given day, any runner, no matter how good or how well prepared, may face unexpected challenges that are hard to overcome.

The weather, technology, other people…these and more can throw a wrench into the best-laid plans, whether you are running a marathon or running a company. There are only so many things you can control in your life; for everything else, you need to have a sense of flexibility. It is also worth noting that you if you spend too much time worrying about backup plans, you may never achieve the goal you set out to accomplish. Plan as best as you can, but always remember than in any complex endeavor, you cannot control everything.

18. Arbitrary Goals Should be Flexible

When I set my Grand Slam goal on my 44th birthday, I told Linh that I would accomplish it by the time I turned 50. As it turned out, I ran at the North Pole and finished the Grand Slam three months after my 50th birthday. My original plan had been to run the North Pole Marathon a year earlier and complete my goal, but I was starting a new business then and did not think I should commit the money for that race since I really did not know what my financial situation would be. I was feeling bad about having to shift my goal until Linh said, "It does not matter when you finish; the only thing that matters is that you DO finish."

He was right, of course. My goal was to do the Grand Slam by 50, but what was so magical about that age? Why not 49, or 51? The only thing special about 50 was that it had a zero on the end. I had looked at a calendar and a list of races and figured it was possible to finish by that age, but there was nothing that said I needed to. The timing was purely arbitrary, and was not the important part of the goal; the important part was to actually run the races. When you set goals, consider what is really important and what is "nice to have" or merely convenient, and realize those latter aspects can change without changing your real objective.

19. Things Often Make More Sense Later

Ever since I began running, there have been things in my professional and personal lives that did not go as planned. At the time I was understandably upset, but as I look back, I realize that if those changes had not happened, I probably never would have done the Grand Slam. Situations such as career changes and choices about where to live ultimately helped me get to the point where I could finish my races. I can see now how something that seemed stressful and unfortunate at the time actually put me on the path to get to where I am today. Sometimes it takes a few years before you can look back and see how all those decisions and events connected to get you to where you are now, but once you can see how it turned out, it all makes sense.

What I realized from this is that when things seem to be going wrong, there is probably a way I can turn the situation into an advantage if I only look hard enough. People like to say things like, "When one door closes, a window opens," but it isn't always obvious; you have to look for the window, and it may take some searching before you find it. There are things that happen outside your control, there are decisions you have to make that you wish you didn't, but when those happen you have the choice of simply being unhappy about it, or making an effort to turn it into something good.

20. How You Train Determines How You Will Perform

An important military concept is to "train like you will fight." The idea behind that is pretty much common sense, that you should simulate the conditions in training that you expect you will have in combat. Runners try to do the same thing, as they train for a certain distance, at a certain pace, with the same clothes and, where possible, in the same weather conditions. One piece of advice often given to runners is that they should start their long training runs at the same time of the morning that their next race will begin, so their body is ready for it. The reality, though, is that life gets in the way, and the best training plans often go out the window when family issues, illness, injuries, weather, and other factors do not cooperate.

Instead of focusing too much on making sure you "train like you fight," realize that you are more likely to "fight like you train." It is good to have an idea of what the actual conditions will be like and try to prepare for them, but on race day it is going to come down to whatever you actually did during your training, all your plans notwithstanding. In that case, it may be more important to focus on fundamentals than on the details. Put more emphasis on running enough miles and less on trying to guess what the race's weather conditions will be. If you are trying to get promoted at work, perhaps spend more time on building your leadership skills and less on mastering technology that might be obsolete in two years anyway. If you have a big presentation, think more about the pace and rhythm of your speaking style and less about finding jokes that are unique to your audience. Make sure the fundamentals are covered, because if you do not have a chance to prepare for everything, the basics will be more important than the smaller details.

21. Remember to Have Fun

In Rio, I stayed a few days after the race so I could enjoy the beaches without worrying that sunburn would affect my running. In Cape Town, I went whale watching and toured wine country. When visiting Paris I got to show it off to a friend who had never visited before, and after the North Pole I met up with an American friend for dinner in Oslo and, a couple days later, had dinner with him again in Stockholm. As I travel I try to balance the demands of the race, the requirements of my job, and my desire to have a good time. Somehow, I manage to achieve all of those pretty well.

Even though these races were part of my journey toward a goal, even though the whole reason I started running marathons was simply to force myself to keep active for my health, I also remember to have fun. One of the great things about running all over the world is the opportunity to visit new places, and early on I decided to take full advantage of that. No matter what goal you are working toward, you need to make sure you never forget to have a good time doing it. Take your vacation days at work, add a weekend onto a business trip in a new city, make a point of joining with other people if that is more fun than doing things on your own, do whatever you have to do. If you are dealing with a crisis or some other tough situation, fun may be the furthest thing from your mind, but even then, be sure to give yourself a break. Generally speaking, if you are working toward something and you are not enjoying your life, you are probably doing it wrong.

22. It Is Usually Better Not to Finish Than It Is Not to Start

So far, I have been lucky on race day, never having been ill or stuck with an injury. There have been a couple races where I was not sure I would finish, but I never had trouble getting started, and that's good. Unless it is going to cause physical injury or other serious complications, I feel like it is better to DNF than to DNS – "Did Not Start." I would rather fail while trying than fail to try. If I do not start, I will always wonder later what would have happened. Imagine flying halfway around the world, not starting for some reason, and then realizing later I probably could have finished. That would be hard to take.

It is easy to decide not to start something if you think there is a good chance you will fail to complete it. The problem with that is, just as things can go disastrously wrong on any given day, so too could things go miraculously right. The only way for that to happen, though, is to get out there and get started. Too many people put something off or decide not to do it because they do not feel confident about their success, but if you don't start, you can never know for sure how it would have turned out. Even if you do not cross the Finish Line, you still earn some sense of victory simply by crossing the Starting Line.

23. It's Not Always About the Time

In my first few races I was determined to get faster each time, and was disappointed when that did not happen. After a couple of years I was trying to crack the 4-hour barrier, and got mad when I could get close but not quite reach it. Once I began traveling around the world for races, I started realizing that maybe sometimes I should just relax and enjoy the setting rather than worrying about my final time. After all, it was not like this was my job. As I got to run more races with Ethan in different countries, I realized that it was ok to just run for fun with a friend without getting too concerned about how fast that run happened. There are times when it is good to focus on the result, and there are other times when it's good to just focus on the experience. My problem for a long time was differentiating between the two, but I think I finally got it.

People who pursue goals tend to be ambitious and interested in self-improvement; if they weren't, they probably would not be pursuing goals. Sometimes, though, it is okay if those goals are not the most important things in front of us. You do not always have to focus on how quickly you reach the Finish Line or how many people you beat getting there. Sometimes just getting to the Starting Line is hard enough, and once you cross it, you can just see what happens without worrying about the result. I have run races specifically to run with a friend, I have run marathons that served as training for other marathons, I have run through cities simply because I would like to see them and this seemed like a good way to take a tour. Every now and then, a run can be just a run.

24. Break Your Memory

I spent a year with a trainer at a gym in Washington DC, and as we began I mentioned that I overpronate when I run, so each of my feet tends to roll inward a bit when they land, rather than coming down straight. This can damage your feet or knees, so it is a good idea to address it. When buying shoes I looked for those that limited pronation, but never thought about how to make it stop. With this knowledge, he had me do some strange walking: first, 25 meters walking on the outside edges of my feet, then back on the inside edges, then repeating the 25 meters on my heels, and finally walking on my toes. The idea was to get past the "muscle memory" that I had developed by running this way for a couple of years. We did this for a few sessions before we ever started working on how my feet should actually land. Before I could get my body to do things differently it first had to forget what it was used to and be open to doing something different.

This sounds like a good idea any time you want to make a big change, whether it's creating healthier habits or taking your company in a new direction. When it comes time to change, you need to consider "breaking the memory." What you do to break that memory does not have to be the same as what you ultimately intend to do. In the case of me and my trainer, walking 25 meters on the sides of my feet was not going to help me finish a marathon, but by getting my feet to "forget" how they landed, it created an opportunity for them to learn how to come down differently. Before trying something new, it helps to forget the old way.

25. Sportsmanship Matters

In June 2015 I had a chance to meet and run with Singapore's men's and women's marathon teams a week before the Southeast Asian Games, and stayed on to watch them race. Soh Rui Yong won the gold with a spectacular finish, and along with his victory, another Singaporean's story emerged. Ashley Liew was running midway in the pack when he suddenly found himself running alone. Some confusion in the race marshaling had caused the leaders to miss a turn, one that Ashley made and which left him in the lead. Looking back and realizing what happened, he slowed until the previous leaders had caught back up to him and everyone was in roughly the same position, and then he took off again.

Goals matter, but it also matters how you achieve them. The cheers of the crowd as you win probably mean very little if there is a voice inside you saying, "You know you didn't win that based on your abilities, right?" Even though it would not have been cheating to keep going forward, Ashley knew that the final result would be based on something other than athletic ability, and that was not what he wanted. It is likely no one would have faulted him had he kept going, but there is a very good chance he would have faulted himself. There is little point in achieving your goals if you have to compromise your integrity to do it.

26. Keep Striving

When I set my Grand Slam goal and planned to accomplish it in a few years, a couple people said, "Wow, that seems fast. What are you going to do when you finish it? You won't have any goals left." I thought that was a silly question. Obviously, once I completed that goal, I would come up with something new. Now that I have finished the Grand Slam, I am aiming to complete another series of races, and I still have some goals focusing on getting faster. Once I achieve those, I will look for some other goals. There is always something else I can do.

Though everyone's goals will depend on what is important to them, I do think everyone should have something in front of them that they aim to accomplish. It keeps life interesting. Sometimes you may only be able to focus on the basics; a person whose immediate goal is to have enough food for the next week may not focus so much on their next overseas marathon. It is exciting, though, to have something positive in front of you that you are working to achieve. Rather than sitting around looking at medals hanging on the wall, I want to go earn some new ones.

26.2 Identify Your Own Lessons

For the final 0.2 of this list, let me suggest that as you run through life, you find your own lessons. This list offers things that have occurred to me, but your life experiences will be different, and so the important lessons from running might be different for you, too. Be very careful about blindly following such personal ideas, because nobody knows you as well as you know yourself.

~ 3 ~
North America
Marine Corps Marathon
Washington DC, USA
October 26, 2008

My journey toward the Marathon Grand Slam started with snow and gray skies at the end of a runway.

I began joining Ethan in January for short runs along parts of the Mount Vernon Trail, starting from the parking lot at an observation area next to National Airport. We would run along the Potomac River in the direction of the District, with the Washington Monument and the US Capitol offering something interesting to look at. The Trail would ultimately become my primary training spot, and though it would be filled at various times of year with rollerbladers as well as cyclists and plenty of runners, everybody got along and there never seemed to be any collisions.

Washington DC in wintertime can be a beautiful place…but it usually isn't. While a blanket of snow falling upon the monuments can look magical, that is not what is typically happening. Instead, we more commonly see gray skies, sleet, biting wind, and an increased number of prescriptions for antidepressants. It gets dark early, so going for a run after work means chasing the last bits of light under a dimming sky. Had I started running by myself, I might not have lasted too long in this environment.

Fortunately, I had company. Ethan always seems to be positive about everything, and his attitude is infectious. Nothing seems to bother him, and any problem can be resolved without stress. He never seemed to mind slowing down to accommodate me. I suppose he might have been going home afterwards and punching the walls, but I have been to his place plenty of times and never saw any holes, so maybe he really is just that relaxed.

He started me out with 3-mile runs. One of the nice things about the Mount Vernon Trail is the set of mile markers along the way, which was great since I was not yet ready to invest in a GPS watch. With the markers it was easy to identify our turnaround point. Three miles was something I knew I could do; one of the many iterations of the Air Force's physical fitness test included a 3-mile run, and I had managed to pass it, so it was distance I knew I could handle.

As much as I appreciated running with Ethan in those first few weeks, I also knew I needed to get out on my own. He had his own goals to accomplish, and I felt like I was slowing him down, so while our evening and weekend runs were great, I needed to shift the schedule around. Fortunately, I realized there was a gym near my office that I could use during the day. Though I was technically assigned to the Pentagon, my office was actually in Crystal City, a mixed commercial and residential neighborhood nearby. Because so many Pentagon offices were located there, the Pentagon Officers Athletic Club – which, despite its traditional name, was open to everyone at the Pentagon – maintained a small annex. The POAC was the first gym I ever joined, but now one of the first things I do when taking a new job or moving to a new city is find a gym nearby.

Joining the POAC meant I had a place to change so I could do a lunchtime run, and my running mood improved as a result. The temperature tended to be warmer, the skies were usually a little clearer, and I could return to work through the afternoon with a clearer head by taking some time to go for a run midday and think through things away from my cubicle. I soon realized that running during the day was good not just for my running, but for my work as well.

A couple of people made this easier to do. During this point in my assignment I was working for Ambassador Charles Ray, who was on loan to us from the State Department, and his senior military officer, Colonel Dave Ellis. They realized that the military personnel in the office were expected to be in a certain physical shape, and so they made fitness part of the job. Their policy was that we could – and, in fact, should – take at least 90 minutes three times a week for exercise. If more leaders had that attitude, they would find themselves with a much healthier and more productive workforce.

Over time, of course, the distance at lunch increased. So as not to abuse the opportunity to get out during the day, I made a point of not going beyond 7 miles, leaving me time to clean up and grab a bite on the way back to the office. Five miles became the normal run, 3-4 times per week. Even now, as I reach the 21-mile point in a marathon, I push myself forward by saying, "C'mon, you've only got a lunchtime run to go." It's funny how early habits will stick in your mind.

As we started to emerge from winter I added Saturday morning runs to my plan. This would be the chance to run longer distances, though for now my idea of a "longer distance" was 8-9 miles. This helped me set a routine for later on, when the weekly long run became the norm. I decided Saturday would be my day to do that because if I was going to give up a weekend night out, it might as well be Friday night when I had been working all day anyway. I would be livelier on Saturday night, so I would save that for going out and head to bed early on Friday.

Moving into springtime, Ethan encouraged me to try running an actual race. I ran the St Paddy's Day 8K on a cold day in March, which was fun, but felt like more of a party in running shorts than a race. The Cherry Blossom 10-Miler, however, was approaching in early April, and this seemed like a perfect opportunity to mix it up with a few thousand other runners. Considering that from the time I started running regularly until the Marine Corps Marathon would be almost ten months, it seemed like a good idea to run some other races along the way to keep my motivation high.

For those who have never seen the cherry blossoms in Washington DC, they are a pretty sight to see. There is a big two-week festival centered around them every year, and the race comes on the weekend in the middle. Of course, you never know for sure if the blossoms will bloom during the festival itself, but in 2008 we got lucky.

The race starts and finishes by the Washington Monument, with a crowd of runners numbering in the thousands. It is a big enough race that they need to start in waves, and I was hoping to run with Ethan and some other folks. We were not able to find each other in advance, though, so I just jumped into my assigned wave toward the back and took off when the time came.

The route is a nice one: moving along some of the major roads and past the Lincoln Memorial, stepping briefly into Virginia, and spending about 4 miles running through East Potomac park, which is very picturesque at that time of year. I remember thinking we were not seeing a whole lot of cherry blossoms during this cherry blossom run, but there were enough to make the name of the race legitimate.

A big reason for running this race was to learn, and I picked up an important lesson near the end. The Finish Line was back near the Washington Monument, and as I ran the last half-mile I let the excitement take over and pushed myself as hard as I could. While that sounds good in theory, the reality was that I was already running a longer distance than I had run before, and the extra speed put additional stress on a body that had not experienced it. Pretty soon after finishing I felt some sharp pain around my left knee, which a little online research revealed was probably an iliotibial band (or IT band) injury. The lesson? It is good to push beyond your previous limits, but you need to build up to it.

Still, I was very pleased with the results. My goal had been to finish this under 9 minutes per mile, and my final time was 1:28:59, so I just made it. I may have had a little trouble lifting my legs to walk, but I could still hold my head up high.

This first race also gave me a sense of how to navigate through crowds and avoid the people who were not too concerned about a fast pace, without adding a lot of extra distance by running around them. I also learned about the extra push you can get when running in front of cheering spectators. It was a lot different running with thousands of others rather than running with one or two friends, or alone, and with a goal of running a long-distance race, some shorter races like this would be a big help.

~

With the 10-Miler behind me it was time to start focusing on running a marathon. I talked with friends and read through various websites to get an idea of what a good training plan looked like, knowing I would ultimately mash it all up into something that worked for me. I needed to factor in things like my work schedule, personal and business travel, changes in the weather through spring and summer, and the need to keep my own motivation up.

I also needed to register for the marathon. In 2008 the Marine Corps Marathon had not quite grown to a size that required a lottery for registration; instead, it was first-come, first-served. While it was certainly possible to sign up online, the organizers hosted an event near the Pentagon when registration opened on April 30th, where runners could sign up in person. There was music, there was a film crew, and as we stood in line and waited for registration to open, it was pretty festive.

Once we were signed up, it was official: I was going to run a marathon. There was really no backing out of it now. I posted it on Facebook, though it was not quite the social media go-to site that it is now; in fact, I may have also posted it on a MySpace page. Mostly, though, I spread the word the old-fashioned way: I talked to people. Quite a few of them did not seem to think I would actually do it, and that only served to increase my determination.

Ethan and I talked about a training plan, though "plan" might be too strong a word for what we came up with. Through online research and conversations with different people I learned about "tapering," the idea that you need to start cutting down your distance a month out from the race so your body is not too wiped out to race well. I learned that when you get close to marathon distance, it takes your body about a day to recover for each mile you ran. In fact, I started learning quite a bit about how the human body works.

Once my knee healed I still had about four months before my taper would start, so I decided to get myself to my maximum distance three times, the final time being a month before the marathon. I also decided that 23 miles would be the farthest I would go in training.

There are two schools of thought on your maximum distance. Some people say you should train at least to 26.2 miles, and perhaps a bit farther, so you know you can do it. Everyone else says to keep it below marathon distance, for a variety of reasons. I chose the latter approach.

My reasoning might not be logical, but it works for me. I got it into my head that 26.2 miles was my goal, and I did not want to achieve it in training; I wanted to hit it when it was for real. While there is nothing magical about 26.2 miles, for me it took on a special meaning, and I decided I would save it for the race. "Besides," I thought, "if I can run 23 miles, I can run 26.2" – or, more accurately, if I could run that far, I could crawl the rest of the way if I had to.

The plan was to run 3-4 times during the week, usually at lunch but sometimes after work, and typically 5-8 miles. These were designed to build up my speed, to see what kind of pace I could get to. Saturdays were the long runs, sometimes with Ethan, sometimes with a group, occasionally alone. These were designed more for endurance, and the idea was to add 3 or 5 miles each week until we hit the max, then back it down and build it up again.

Washington DC is not know for having cool summers, so as we moved into the season, and as our long runs got longer, we started meeting earlier and earlier on Saturdays. This was not something I had really planned on, and as someone who is definitely not a morning person, it sometimes offered a bigger challenge than the distance we were running that day. Ultimately, though, I made it on time, and I stuck with the plan throughout the months that followed.

The summer of 2008 was a period when I started developing better habits and stronger self-discipline, and at age 42, it was about time. Many of the good practices I used during my doctoral studies a few years earlier seemed to have faded into the mist, and it was time to bring them back into the light of day. There was a lot going on in my life – work, friends, dating someone new, and now running – and it was important to strike a balance.

Obviously, having an upcoming marathon provided most of the motivation, and training with others helped because it meant I made a commitment to join them and could not just turn off the alarm and go back to sleep. Small rewards helped, too. I had discovered the cinnamon rolls of a nearby bakery, which pretty much seemed to have been baked by angels, and I told myself I could have one after I finished my Saturday run. After my first 23-mile run I let myself have a large café mocha immediately after finishing. I told the barista I had earned it since I had just run 23 miles, but she seemed unimpressed.

Cinnamon rolls and café mochas aside, I did find myself eating better during this period, too. I was deciding on dinner based on whether or not I was running the next day, and if so, how far. I had already stopped drinking sugared sodas long before, but now found myself drinking a lot more water and less diet soft drinks. Though I lost some more weight, I also learned that training for a marathon is not an ideal strategy for weight loss. While there is certainly a lot more exercise, you also end up eating more so you have the energy to run. Training like this can help you if you have a lot to lose, I think, but if you are trying to drop the "final five," they may not melt off like you planned.

~

Being a military officer, I would regularly get some sort of medical exam each year, though it was usually pretty basic. 2008 was different, because I was about to participate in an overseas program that required a more detailed checkup. So, I spent a couple days at the Pentagon Clinic filling up some cups and syringes, and answering a bunch of questions.

When I returned to get the results one afternoon in July, the doctor stared at the computer screen for a bit, then casually looked at me over his shoulder and said, "Hey, did you know it looks like you have colon cancer?" Um, no. No I did not. I am guessing "bedside manner" was not his biggest strength on his most recent performance review.

I was pretty stunned by the news, to say the least. Here I was, finally taking a big step toward improving my health and fitness, a few months from running my first marathon, and he is telling me I may have a life-threatening illness? I realize that good things and bad things in life often seem to balance each other, but this seemed ridiculous.

The uncertainty added a lot to my stress. If I had at least known one way or the other, I could have made some decisions. The ironic thing was, the symptoms I was experiencing could also have been caused by my running. It was possible that my body was responding to the increased mileage and other changing habits, and producing a result that confused the doctors. As it was, I would need a colonoscopy to check things out, and the military medical system did not seem to be in a hurry to get me scheduled.

Fortunately a cancellation occurred, and three weeks later I had an appointment at the Walter Reed Army Medical Center. The date is easy to remember: August 8, 2008, or 08/08/08, which was the opening day of the Beijing Olympic Games. My friend Stan arranged to be at the hospital to bring me home, since with the sedatives they were unwilling to let me drive myself. Apparently we went to lunch afterwards at my favorite restaurant, a fact that I only realized a couple months later when I asked if he had ever been there. He got a strange look on his face, before repeating to me all the secrets I had shared with him during our lunch. I learned to be careful with sedatives, because they will mess with your mind, not to mention your inhibitions.

While the procedure was not especially pleasant, it also was not especially memorable. The drugs they gave me left me drifting in and out of consciousness, so I did not really notice much until I was in the recovery room. I rested awhile until the doctor came back with the report, and started reeling off a variety of medical terms and telling me how the procedure went. I finally put my hand on his arm until he stopped talking, looked him in the eye, and asked very deliberately, "Do I have cancer?" "Oh," he said, "no, you don't. You're fine."

It would be an understatement to merely say I was relieved. This episode reinforced my belief that I should be getting out and doing the things I was thinking about, because we really never know how much time we have left. Though I was already moving in that direction, with the marathon as well as other plans for the future, this scare convinced me that waiting around for the right time to do something was not a great idea. It's better to make "now" the right time.

After getting the clean bill of health from my doctors, I had one last dress rehearsal. Following Ethan's advice I had registered for the Army 10-Miler, taking place three weeks before I would run the marathon. This race would start and end at the Pentagon and cover some of the same route as the marathon, adding some more knowledge to what I had experienced during the Cherry Blossom 10-Miler months earlier.

This time around, with the big race coming only a few weeks later, I was determined not to injure myself. I avoided pushing myself too hard, and instead focused on techniques such as my stride and my breathing. I also paid attention to the layout of the starting area and certain spots along the route, such as the 14th Street Bridge, which I would see again in three weeks' time. It was a good opportunity to get out and practice again in an actual race environment, and despite holding back, I finished more than six minutes faster than my previous 10-mile race six months earlier. I guess I had been doing something right during all that time.

~

Finally, it was race day. When October 28th arrived, I was ready to go. I crashed at Stan's place the night before, and he drove me to the nearby Metro station so I could travel the two stops to the runners' area at the Pentagon. I knew that making things easier in the morning would reduce some of the stress I felt before the race, so I tried to plan things in advance as best as I could. My theory was that by controlling the things that I could, I would have more time to deal with the things that I couldn't.

It was easy to find the right crowd to follow; the train was full of people in running shorts with numbers pinned to their shirts. With a couple of races behind me, I knew the routine and started aiming for the baggage trucks. I was trying to find Ethan and the others before dropping off my phone. Despite the advantages of modern technology, we still had to locate each other among tens of thousands of runners and their supporters. Fortunately, the baggage trucks were numbered based on our bibs, and we figured it out using those.

We found a spot to stretch and jog a bit, just to warm things up. The day was cool and a little cloudy, which seemed like perfect marathon weather. It was a bit of a hike to the starting corral so we followed the masses and found our spot. The starting area was large so we did not have the cramped feeling I experienced at the earlier races in the year. It was so big, in fact, that even after the gun went off it was about 10 minutes before we actually crossed the Starting Line.

As we got started I was surprised by the number of people who immediately ran off the course and into the trees by the side of the road. It had not occurred to me as we gathered in the corrals that you need to moderate your pre-race hydration. Drink more water than you need, and it will pass through your system and hit your bladder. Once it gets there, there is only one way out, and it's not through sweating. I laughed at first, but that laughter would come back to haunt me later in the morning.

The race started out through Arlington, where the spectators were already out, and soon enough took us back to the Key Bridge and into the District itself. Ethan had told me not to set my expectations for the race based on these first few miles, since the hour was early, the crowd of fans was small, and the runners were pretty packed together. As we stepped across the bridge I was feeling good, fairly peaceful and just enjoying the experience. The adrenaline rush would come later.

Once across the bridge we turned left, away from the retail area of Georgetown, with the university up to our right and the Potomac River on our left. I had trained along running paths in the area, but this was my first time along the roads, so it was still new territory. I knew from the map, though, that we would soon be running through residential neighborhoods, and pretty quickly after that we would be along the very busy area of M Street.

Passing by some trees before we started running among the houses, Ethan said, "This is our last chance to pee if you have to." I had not thought about that before seeing the crowd at the Starting Line, but now I realized he had a point. I had been drinking every chance I had, but since the temperature was still low I had not sweated it all out, and I needed to get rid of the excess water in my system. Once we got past the trees we would be running in front of spectators for most of the rest of the race. As a military officer with a couple deployments I had learned that when you have a chance to do something, you should do it, because you never know when you will get the chance again. So, off we headed to the tree line, along with dozens of other runners.

M Street was the point where the rowdies started coming out. It was here that we started seeing more signs and hearing more noise, and this offered a good boost. I realized that not wanting to look bad in front of others offered some motivation to run strong, and I decided to make use of that for the rest of the race.

The halfway point is something that will always stick with me. As we rounded Hains Point and passed the 13-mile marker, I said to Ethan,

"You know, the winners are already done." Without missing a beat, he replied, "Don't worry about them. Run your own race." That was great advice then, it is great advice now, and it applies across all aspects of life, not just running. In a world of saturated social media and constant updates about what others are doing, it is good if we set our own standards for success in life, and work hard toward those instead of always being concerned that we are missing out on something.

It was only a few minutes later that Ethan put that advice into practice. As we approached the Lincoln Memorial, he told me to go on ahead. We had discussed this; Ethan had an issue with one leg that would probably start bothering him around 16 miles into the race, and it was just about that time. As much as I wanted to run with him, he realized that if I had the ability to keep running while he needed to walk a bit, I would be disappointed if I didn't keep moving. He told me to go, so I went.

Running around the Lincoln Memorial we were once again making our way through a large audience, and things got very, very loud for the first time. Unlike some of the other areas of the course, this part got a little narrow, so the crowds were right in our ears. For whatever reason, the image of running through this point has always stuck with me, maybe because I had never, ever had so many people cheering me on in an athletic event before. Whatever the reason, it was certainly rejuvenating.

Past the Memorial, we soon found ourselves on Constitution Avenue, which carried us up along the National Mall and the various Smithsonian museums, toward the US Capitol building, then back down Independence Avenue on the other side. It got loud here again, as the Mall is well served by Metro stations and it was easy for people to come out and cheer on their friends, family members, and random strangers. This was the first place I saw someone I knew, as Stan was out there yelling and taking pictures. That helped a lot.

Coming through the National Mall area left me pretty pumped up, and I have to tip my hat to the race organizers, because the next couple of miles required that rush. Turning away from the Mall and toward the 14th Street Bridge, the sounds of the crowd started to fade, and I knew it would be quiet for a while. Without easy access to the bridge, most spectators stayed away. A few people with bikes were along the route, but for the most part the only people we saw were other runners.

That created an interesting challenge, as we were now at about the 18-mile point, which for many people is where they hit "the wall." Having only run in 10-mile races before this, I had experienced the wall only in training. Now, with an actual Finish Line somewhere ahead of me, the wall took on greater importance. Fortunately, I had run across this bridge just a few weeks earlier during the Army 10-Miler, so at least I was on familiar territory, and I think that helped reduce the psychological impact of what my body was starting to tell me.

With my goal of not walking at all, and with Ethan's reminder to "run your own race," I ignored the many people who started walking at this point, and just kept running forward. The bridge proved to be a good learning experience, as I had never really noticed that bridges are curved like a hill rather than straight. Maybe everyone else knows that bridges are built that way, sloping upward to the halfway point before dropping down again, but I never noticed. After today, I would never forget it.

Coming across the bridge we moved into Crystal City, the commercial and residential area where I worked and where I started my long runs every Saturday. At this point we were about 20 miles into the race and I felt myself climbing over the wall. The streets were pretty full because this was an out and back route through the neighborhood; we went in about a mile and a half, did a U-turn, and came out again. With the Metro station there, plenty of people made this a point to come and see their friends and family, and the band playing there added to the noise of the crowd.

I saw Stan again around here, both coming into and leaving the neighborhood. Despite the crowds in the Metro system, he had made his way here before I arrived. That was the perfect place to get a thumbs-up from him, as we were coming through the 21- and 22-mile markers, and I was definitely feeling the effects of the day. It was also the last time I would see anyone I knew until the Finish Line.

Heading out of Crystal City I was feeling pretty energized, knowing that I was going to be able to do this. I had gotten over the wall and found my second wind, and I was not going to be stopped. Passing by the Pentagon for the second time that day, I saw the 24-mile marker and was amazed by how much energy I still had. Of course, realizing that I only had two miles to go probably had something to do with that.

What I had not counted on was how quiet and lonely the final couple of miles would be. As I moved along the same stretch of road where I had started a few hours earlier, there were almost no spectators, and not that many other runners around me. For those that I did encounter, there were smiles and nods as we passed each other, but by this point nobody was in the mood for conversation.

I had never actually seen where the Finish Line was. I knew it was at the Marine Corps War Memorial – the famous Iwo Jima statue – but I did not review the layout before the race. As I moved down the road I could see a crowd ahead along one side, and I realized that must be the turnoff to the final climb and the Finish Line. What I had not counted on was just how big that crowd would be.

The Finish Line was at the top of a slope, with bleachers near the line, but the crowd was much too big to be constrained in that area. Plenty of people had moved down the hill and were along the road, so what I thought was the turnoff was merely the beginning of a very, very large audience. As I started running past the crowd, with their cheering and noisemakers and signs, I picked up the pace because I figured I was almost done. After a while I was asking myself, "Where is the turn?," because the crowd seemed to go on and on and on. It would be bad to waste my final energy on a long stretch of flat road when I still had a hill coming up.

Finally, I saw it: the Mile 26 sign, and just beyond, the balloons marking the left turn. Rounding the curve and seeing the hill in front of me, I knew this was the time to use it all up and finish the race with nothing left in the tank. I made a strong push as I moved around the curves on my way up, and suddenly saw in front of me a huge banner stretching over the road. With a yell as I ran past the grandstand, I crossed the Finish Line 4 hours, 36 minutes, and 53 seconds after starting.

That time, 4:36:53, was not going to get me into any hall of fame, but at that point I absolutely did not care. I entered the race with a few goals: finish without injury, no walking, and complete it in less than five hours. Check, check, and check.

Standing there on that hilltop, having my photo taken in front of the memorial, a medal hanging around my neck, I could not believe what I had just done. I had been a kid with no athletic ability whatsoever. I had been a university student who could count on both hands the number of times I stepped into the gym. I had been a military officer who had done the bare minimum when it came to maintaining my fitness.

Now, I was a marathoner.

~ 4 ~
Asia
Standard Chartered Singapore Marathon
Singapore
December 7, 2008

Many of the great things happening in 2008 actually got their start back in 2007.

My return from Afghanistan led to more than just me starting to run. Soon after getting back from there, a random meeting at an academic conference put me on a path that changed my life in many ways. One of those changes, as it happens, was the chance to become an international marathoner.

A few years earlier I had become a member of an academic association with the unwieldy name of the Inter-University Seminar on Armed Forces and Society. IUSAFS is the professional association for academics who study the military and, in particular, a military's relationship with the rest of its nation's population. I had joined them while teaching at the Air Force Academy, and had not only maintained my membership in the group, but would also be chairing a panel on counterinsurgency and delivering a paper at their 2007 conference in Chicago.

These conferences were a great opportunity to stay connected with my former colleagues from the Air Force Academy and West Point, and it was during a chat with an Army colleague that I was introduced to a professor from Nanyang Technological University in Singapore. He taught there in the S. Rajaratnam School of International Studies, which had recently evolved from a research center into a degree-granting graduate school. I had used research from their center before and was familiar with a number of the people on the faculty, and I had been to Singapore once before and enjoyed it, so I jokingly told him, "If you guys ever need a visiting professor, give me a call." Little did I know how that one comment would change the course of my life.

Once I was back to the Pentagon and reviewing my notes, I thought about that brief introduction and started wondering about teaching overseas. Years earlier I had considered applying to be a Fulbright Scholar, but my deployment to Iraq had messed that up and I never pursued it. For an American academic, teaching as a Fulbright is a chance to introduce American styles of teaching into an overseas classroom while opening a dialogue that increases understanding on both sides. As a program sponsored by the US Department of State, it offers a great way to learn from other cultures while helping them learn about how we do things in the US, and it always seemed like it would be very rewarding. Considering that much of my work during my Pentagon assignment dealt with Southeast Asia, it would have been interesting and educational to spend some time there.

Even though I knew the application deadline had passed while I was in Afghanistan, I pulled up the Fulbright website just to see what opportunities had been out there this year. One in particular caught my eye: the Rajaratnam School at Nanyang Technological University was looking for a professor to teach a course on US national security policy in their master's degree program, and even though the deadline had been months earlier, the opportunity was still open because they had not gotten a viable candidate. I figured the definition of "a viable candidate" might include a Pentagon staff officer with a PhD in public policy and 7 years of teaching national security policy combined with two wartime deployments. A quick email to the Fulbright Commission confirmed that I would be the kind of person they had in mind, and with the approval of my bosses, I submitted my application.

Months later I was accepted, and learned I would be going to Singapore in November 2008 for four months. At that point I had to start the process of getting the Department of Defense's paperwork done. Considering the Fulbright program is sponsored by another government agency you would not think this would be a problem, but I am pretty sure we landed people on the Moon with less bureaucracy than I faced.

Fortunately, my boss at the Pentagon had been the US ambassador to Cambodia, where he was a big fan of the Fulbright program. He and our senior military officer quickly signed all the letters I needed them to sign. Both Ambassador Ray and Colonel Ellis recognized the value of having an officer teaching in an academic program like this in a country that was America's most important military partner in Southeast Asia, so with their support, everything finally worked.

As the summer of 2008 progressed, I was training hard for the Marine Corps Marathon and feeling pleased with the changes I was seeing in myself. I was also getting excited about the event itself, and for the first time started wondering if I should think about doing more marathons. After all, this was a lot of work for just one race, so maybe I should consider doing some others, too. I started wondering about the marathons that would be taking place in Asia during my Fulbright experience.

A quick check online showed that I was in luck. The Standard Chartered Singapore Marathon would be held in December, and registration was still open. As an added bonus, the Standard Chartered Hong Kong Marathon was set for February, giving me a chance to run through that city before I returned to the US the following month. Now registered for three marathons in three countries in the coming months, I was starting to feel like a super-marathoner even though I had yet to run even one.

Left unspoken through all of this was the fact that the Singapore race would be six weeks after the Marine Corps Marathon, and the Hong Kong race would be nine weeks later. Three marathons in 15 weeks is not a great plan for most people, and for someone preparing for his first race, it was probably an extremely bad idea. The conventional wisdom is that it takes your body about a month to recover from a marathon, so if you want to have a month for recovery, a month to train up again, and a month to taper off, neither six weeks nor nine weeks is really enough time. Yes, there are people who take on extreme challenges, like a marathon every week for a year, or 7 marathons on 7 continents in 7 days, but those are the outliers. For most runners, a minimum of three months between races is probably a good idea. Fortunately, I was too dumb to realize that.

~

About ten days after finishing my first marathon, I boarded a flight to start the 24-hour journey to Singapore. I was excited about the chance to live overseas for the first time, to get back into the classroom, and to learn more about Southeast Asian cultures and politics so I could do my Pentagon job better. I sensed a lot of potential in this adventure.

For the first few days, I also sensed a lot of disorientation. If God created the Earth, then the Devil created jet lag. Fortunately, I had a little over week until my first class, so I had time to take care of basic logistical tasks while wandering around in a daze. One of those tasks was to find a gym.

I had spent 2008 just running, not giving much thought to weight training. Though I had joined the Pentagon gym near my office, it was simply to have a place to change clothes when I went for a run at lunch. I really never considered lifting weights. After all, I was trying to run fast, not lift heavy things; I wanted to be The Flash, not Superman.

Throughout the year, though, many of the runners I knew also spent time in the gym, and I started wondering about the benefits. As I was running the later miles of the Marine Corps Marathon and started feeling intense pain in body parts that I never realized had nerve endings, I began to think that if my muscles were stronger I might not be feeling this. I decided that, among all the other new things I would do in Singapore, I would also join a gym and work on building up my strength.

Once I got settled into my apartment I checked out the local area and found a gym in a nearby shopping center. It was not quite the atmosphere I had in mind – it was in the basement, so there was no natural light and it just seemed dark throughout – but it was a 3-minute walk from my apartment, and I knew convenience would help get me there regularly. I was already commuting about 45 minutes to the university, so adding commuting time for the gym could easily keep me from going.

When I went to ask them about a membership, I was introduced to the very common Singaporean character trait of sticking to the rules no matter what. I explained I would be in town for four months and would like a membership, and was told, "There is a one-year minimum." I repeated I would only be there for four months and was told again, "One year." I asked, "Would you rather have my money for four months, or not at all?," and the reply was simply "One year." I realize that following policies even when they don't make sense is not unique to Singapore, but this first exposure to it has, over the years, made me recognize how that philosophy unnecessarily complicates day-to-day life there.

Unwilling to pay for eight months of a gym membership that I would not use, I retreated to my laptop and found California Fitness, which had four gyms on the island. A note to them explaining my situation got a quick response from the membership manager who said, "We would be happy to do a shorter membership; come on over!" I went to their flagship gym on Orchard Road, Singapore's glitzy shopping street, and found a multi-story gym with much more equipment than I could ever use, and members who looked like they knew what they were doing.

I spoke with the membership manager who then asked one of the trainers to give me a tour. Mattew – and no, that is not a typo, he does not use an "h" in his name – showed me around and, more importantly, asked me about my goals. I think that is pretty important, since there is no point in trying to sell someone on features that do not align with their objectives. I had been thinking about working with a trainer, since I had no idea what to do in the gym, so I told Mattew that I was a runner who needed to be in shape for that. He started talking about core strength, balance, and proper center of gravity, and I knew I had found my trainer.

With the gym settled, my living situation all set, and my work starting off smoothly, it was time to start thinking seriously about the marathon coming up in a few weeks. I was at the gym twice a week with Mattew and once a week on my own, and every session included at least half an hour on the treadmill. That was kind of fun; the treadmills were arranged facing floor-to-ceiling windows on the ground floor, so to people passing by we were like animals in a zoo. Watching them walk past with ice cream cones from a nearby shop helped push me to improve my fitness so that I, too, could eat ice cream without feeling guilty. Ultimately, though, I needed to get off the treadmill and get out onto the road.

~

There are many positive things to say about Singapore, but in those four months that I was living there, "a runner's paradise" did not seem to be one of them. In addition to having a new work schedule and trying to find my way around in a new culture, I also had the problem of finding a place to actually run.

I was teaching at Nanyang Technological University, on the western side of the island, and living in Chinatown, which is more centrally located. The result was a 45-minute commute by train and bus each way, which meant I was often getting home after dark. I was in a highly urbanized neighborhood with narrow sidewalks, and there really was no place to run near my home. Unlike when I lived in Washington, I did not have a car that I could drive to find someplace else, and I would not have known where to go even if I did. The solution, then, was to run at the university.

Running at the school turned out to be an excellent idea. The wide roads wound through the campus, and by the time I ran in the evening there was very little foot traffic on the sidewalks or cars on the road.

There was a little-used athletic center that offered a convenient place to change. There were a lot of hills, affording me my first opportunity to try training that way.

Mentally, it was a great release. This was my first time back in the classroom after a couple of years, and I really wanted to make a good impression, so I was a bit stressed trying to make everything perfect. This was also a very different teaching environment for me; my students from Asia, which included 22 of the 24 in my class, told me their educational upbringing was one of listening to a lecturer, writing down everything they said, then repeating it on an exam. That is not at all the style of teaching I use, so the struggle between what I wanted them to do and what they were used to was taking a lot of effort. Going for a run at the end of the day offered a way to clear my head before commuting home.

I rarely saw other runners around the campus, and this reinforced the idea that Singapore did not have much of a running culture. With so many students living on campus, I thought I would see more of them out in the evening. Given the open nature of the campus, I also thought plenty of off-campus students and faculty would take advantage of being here and go for a run before heading home to their built up neighborhoods and heavily-trafficked streets.

When I would come across the occasional runner other than myself, I noticed something odd. My experience in the US was that, when runners passed each other, we would give each other a nod or a "hello." Here, though, other runners averted their eyes and seemed to ignore each other. A local friend later told me that people tend not to make eye contact with strangers here. His story was that years ago, when criminal gangs were common in Singapore, making eye contact with a gangster was a good way to get beaten up, and over time people developed the habit of simply not looking strangers in the eye when passing them. Whatever the reason, it strengthened my perception that runners here did not comprise a community in the way that I was used to.

In the meantime, my work at the gym continued, and I was seeing progress. At one point I mentioned to Mattew that the washer and dryer in my apartment seemed to be shrinking my shirts, because they were getting tighter. He looked at me strangely and pointed out that maybe my body was getting bigger as a result of working hard in the gym for a few weeks. That honestly had not occurred to me.

I cannot overemphasize the importance of my experience with the gym in Singapore. Beyond the physical benefits, there was also a sense of accountability that filled the gap left by not having Ethan as a running partner. There would be no skipping out of the gym when I had a trainer waiting for me. Even on the days I was working out on my own, Mattew would often check my weights or my form, even if he was just walking past me with another client. Over time, the gym also offered a source of community in an unfamiliar city, as I would see the same people regularly and start feeling accepted, especially when I showed up after the marathon in my Finisher's t-shirt and started getting compliments from other members.

Ultimately, though, it all came down to running. Putting my full effort into teaching and taking on new challenges in the gym meant I had to get even better at personal planning and making the time to run the roads and clock the miles I needed to get ready during that first month in Singapore.

~

Finally, it was race day. Though I vaguely knew where to go to find the starting area, based on the race's website, I still did not know my way around Singapore. My plan was to give a taxi driver the destination and let him figure it out. Whether he was equally confused, or my accent made it hard to understand me, I will never know, but in any case he headed in the wrong direction. Even though I did not know where we were, I knew the trip was taking much longer than it should, and I finally got him to stop so we could figure it out.

Arriving at the drop-off point at the War Memorial, I realized I still was not sure where to go, so I just started following the crowd. The starting area itself was on a bridge, away from any of the mass transit points and a bit of a walk from where we were. Thousands of us gathered not far from the Fullerton Hotel, one of Singapore's more historic (and expensive) hotels. The emcee at the starting area encouraged us to send a "wakeup call" to the guests, who at this point were probably regretting taking rooms there on this particular weekend.

Having studied statistics in graduate school, I know that a sample size of 1 does not give you much in the way of useful information. With that in mind, I should have anticipated a lot of differences between this race and the only marathon I had run before, and perhaps even approached it as if it was my first one. About the only thing that was the same as the Marine Corps Marathon was the distance, and even that was measured in kilometers rather than miles.

The race started at 5:30am, so I had been up since about 3 and managed to find everything in the dark. The logic behind the early start was simple: it would allow us to run for about an hour and a half before the sun came up. The importance of that became very clear to me later that morning.

Singapore is an extremely organized place, so the gun went off exactly on time, and we moved out. One interesting element here was that there would be other events going on as well – a half-marathon and a 10K – and though they would start later than we did, we would all finish at the same point. The different starting times and different routes were designed to avoid overlapping each other, at least until the end, but it meant that instead of just the roughly 13,000 marathoners, there would be a total of about 50,000 people participating during the day.

We started out with a short run toward the southwest, before turning to the east. The course was largely an out-and-back, with a U-turn just before the halfway point. About 7 miles into the race we entered East Coast Park, where we would spend the next 10 miles. The way the course looped meant I got to see the leaders running past me in the other direction. It was the last time I would see them until their photos were in the newspaper the next day.

As we ran east we were watching the sun climb above the horizon, and even that early in the race my body was telling me that I needed to get as much of this done as I could before sunrise. The race is held in December because this is supposed to be the coolest time of the year, but when you are only one degree off the equator, it's going to be hot no matter what day it is. Fortunately, soon after the sun rose we hit the U-turn and I was able to put it to my back, so that helped a little.

As in the Marine Corps Marathon, I still was not in the habit of wearing a stopwatch. Unlike that race, though, in this one there were no clocks along the way, so I had no idea what my pace was. Even if I had worn a watch, I would have to translate the kilometer markers into miles, because I still was not used to thinking that way. I realize, of course, that pretty much everyone in the world besides the United States measures in kilometers rather than miles, but I had not yet trained my brain to think like that.

The drink stations were positioned roughly a mile apart, usually with a choice of water and a sports drink. I tried alternating between the two, but the sports drink was not one of the American brands I was used to, and this was the first time I had tried it. Drinking something for the first time on race day is not the smartest thing to do, because you do not know how your body will react to it.

Whether or not it was due to the new sports drink, I definitely starting feeling a little heavy in my stomach. I thought that perhaps I was overhydrating, a common response by runners in a hot and unfamiliar environment, so I started watering only at every other station. Looking back on it, that might have been a bad idea, and I realized when I had some difficulties later that perhaps the problem was not overhydrating, but overheating. Chalk that up as a lesson learned about running marathons in the tropics: it is very unlikely that you are drinking too much water.

The weirdest thing about this race for me was that there was no crowd, practically no one out there along the route, until we approached the Finish Line. There were a couple of secondary school drum corps along the way, a few cheerleaders at one section of East Coast Park, and a small collection of family members and friends, but even some of the volunteers working along the route were napping. This was nothing like what I had experienced in Washington, and I felt like I was missing something because I know what a crowd can do to help motivate you, and was kind of expecting it.

It seemed obvious to me that the lack of spectators probably had something to do with the early start, but even later in the morning, there were very few people out there, certainly nothing like the 100,000 people or so in Washington. I figured the lack of accessibility was also a factor, since very few points along the route were close to train stations. One possibility had not occurred to me, though, until I was talking with an Australian tourist afterwards on the train heading home and he asked, "Well, marathons aren't really a spectator sport, are they?" This was the first time I considered that coming out and watching thousands of people run past, hoping for a brief glimpse of someone you know, might be a uniquely American thing.

As we exited East Coast Park and moved along the final 7 miles or so, the heat really started taking its toll. My lower back was seriously hurting, and I was starting to get dehydration symptoms such as tingling hands and mild stomach cramps, neither of which is a good sign. I could feel my speed dropping, and then I did the thing I did not want to do: I started walking. For about a mile I alternated between walking and jogging. I realized that my original fear was true: once I start walking, I will have a hard time running again, and it would be a real challenge to get back to the speed I had earlier. A subconscious sense of "what's the point?" seemed to invade my mind.

To counter the heat, Singapore offered something I found especially useful: sponges. Volunteers at some of the later water stations were handing us sponges soaked in water that most of us applied to the backs of our necks before squeezing them until empty over our heads. Just after this, though, was a wonderful invention I would love to see at every race: a structure with hoses mounted on it, offering us a water spray through which we could run. That was useful, and it re-energized me and helped me get back to running.

I felt better during the last few miles, even though I had realized I would be slower than my Marine Corps Marathon time. Once I hit the 42km marker I gave it everything I had for the final 200 meters and ran in for a nice finish, but my back was hurting so much after crossing the line that I made my way over to a barrier in the finish area and leaned against it. Three medical volunteers came out of nowhere and had me sit down and straighten my legs, but offered no water, which I would have thought would be a good first step. I think they were all set to do something to my legs until I said the problem was my lower back and they all stepped away; I guess their training did not extend to that.

My final time was 4:55:17, almost 19 minutes slower than the Marine Corps Marathon. However, given everything that had happened in the six weeks since my last marathon – moving to a new country, starting a new temporary job, trying to find a place to run – I was just happy that I finished. Come to think of it, I was just happy that I started. I ended up as number 2,659 out of 12,393 finishers, which put me in the 79th percentile, and I felt like that was still pretty good. The heat was a real issue for me, but perhaps it was an issue for the local runners, too.

Oddly enough, I ran faster in the second ten kilometers than in the first ten. Part of that may have been that the runners were still crowded for the first few kilometers, or it may have been that I started running faster when the sun started coming up and I could see where I was going. Once the sun was overhead, though, everything slowed down. I never ran at my Marine Corps Marathon pace, though of course, I ran the first

16 miles of that race with Ethan while this one was on my own. I am sure that made a difference.

I made it into the finish area, turned in my timing chip and got my finisher's shirt and medal, then wandered around looking for something to drink. I ended up sitting down at a volunteer table with tingling, dizziness, and a slightly swollen tongue making it difficult to speak. I had trouble explaining to the young nursing student volunteers why I was sitting there, but they brought me some water and kept an eye on me. A lady sat next to me who had just completed her first half-marathon, and who was also a teacher like me, so we chatted about teaching in Singapore and about her son's experiences studying and then working as a consultant in New York. I waited there about 20 minutes with some water until the blue spots in front of my eyes went away, and by then I was ready to make my way home.

Nine weeks later I would cash in some frequent flyer miles and head for the slightly cooler temperatures of Hong Kong for the marathon there, and my results were surprising. On the final turn toward the Finish Line at Victoria Park, I saw the clock and realized I was on track for a new record. With a burst of speed in the final 200 meters, I finished with a time of 4:34:04, setting a new personal best that was more than 2 minutes faster than my Marine Corps Marathon time. My problems in Singapore were most likely not due to issues with my fitness, nor with the fact that I had recently run a marathon; instead, it really seemed to be the climate.

Beware the heat in Singapore; it is not for the weak.

~ 5 ~
Europe
Marathon de Paris
Paris, France
April 10, 2011

The 28 months between my second continent and my third one were anything but boring.

While I had been in Singapore for my Fulbright, I had gotten word from Colonel Ellis at the Pentagon that, based on the promotion recommendation I got from the Assistant Secretary of Defense who was above me, I would most likely be getting promoted to the rank of colonel. This put me in an interesting position, as my plan had been to retire from the Air Force in 2010. I had even shared this plan with the leadership in my organization so they would not expend any political capital trying to get me promoted. None was needed, though, as someone apparently saw potential in me.

I will not lie; this was a surprise. I had spent my career taking assignments that looked interesting and provided an opportunity where my talents could make a difference. What I had not been doing was taking assignments that would help me get promoted along the traditional path. There had been one squadron commander's position for which I had applied, but my heart was not in it; the role would have been more bureaucratic than operational, and I was not in the mood for that. I had told a 2-star general that I did not want to be his aide-de-camp because my skills could be put to better use doing the organization's mission rather than being his personal assistant. I had earned my PhD, which I had been told was the kiss of death for career progression.

Still, someone obviously felt I had something to offer. Though I was never told what led to the recommendation that I received, my sense was that the Assistant Secretary, being a civilian, was looking for different qualities than a career military officer might. Whatever drove his decision, it would probably force me to make a decision, too, in 2009.

Sure enough, on June 23rd I got the official word from Ambassador Ray that I had been selected for promotion. The way the military works, a promotion board selects a large group of officers at once, but they have to space out the actual promotions to the new rank over an extended period of time. Since we don't need a few hundred new colonels all at once, the promotions are timed to coincide with retirements of other colonels as well as promotions of some colonels to become generals. The timing is based on seniority, and as a result it would be a year before I would pin on the insignia of my new rank.

One advantage of having that much time is that it gave me an opportunity to search for a new assignment. I had told friends that I would put off my retirement if I found an assignment that would make use of my skills, but if I got something that just seemed irrelevant, I would hold to my original plan to retire. I had never expected to become a colonel, and making it to a particular rank was never a goal of mine. All I wanted was an interesting career and a chance to offer something useful, and as long as I had the opportunity to do that, I would stick around.

In the meantime, I kept running. While I was in Singapore I started looking for other marathons that I could run as soon as I got back to the US, but my friends dissuaded me from that. They made the point – and it was a good one – that I could easily burn out quickly if I ran too many too soon. They were right, of course; running 2-3 per year would be a little more normal.

But there are plenty of shorter races that are a lot of fun, so I went for those. I decided to once again run the St Paddy's Day 8K soon after returning from Singapore, and this time I got Stan to run with me. In April I took on the Cherry Blossom 10-Miler again; I had literally been sitting at my computer in Singapore waiting for the moment that registration opened, knowing that it fills up quickly. I managed to shave a minute and a half off my previous 10-mile time, and a few months later I ran the Army 10-Miler again, speeding up by another 30 seconds.

I was pleased with the progress I was seeing, and I had continued not only my running once I returned, but also my strength training in the gym. Mattew had written out some routines for me to use, to keep building my core strength in particular. My running distances had increased to the point that my lunchtime runs tended to be around 7 miles and my weekend runs typically did not get below half-marathon distance.

One day in the spring I saw a practical impact of everything I had been doing, and I also saw a sign of just how cocky I was getting about all this. Each year I was required to take a physical fitness test, which for the Air Force now consisted of sit ups, pushups, and a 1.5-mile run, along with some other measurements. My annual test was approaching in late March, but I asked to hold off until after the Cherry Blossom 10-Miler. I explained that I was training for a distance race and that a 1.5-mile sprint would not be helpful right now. The sergeant overseeing the test commented that she had never heard 1.5 miles referred to as a "sprint" before, but there was no problem delaying for a month.

Once I finally got around to taking the test, I knocked out the right number of pushups and sit ups to get the maximum points. I went to the run with a perfect score, and took off along the outdoor track to complete the timed run with a couple of younger people. Hearing the sergeant call out the times as I finished, I realized I had achieved the maximum points in this element of the test, too. At age 43, I had finally gotten a perfect score on my physical fitness test, an accomplishment that rivaled running a marathon. I had gone from someone who had trouble even passing the test to someone who had aced it. I was in the best shape of my life, and it seemed like it would only get better.

As we got into autumn, my future career as an officer and my future abilities as a runner were both taking shape. I had reached out to a faculty member at the National Defense University about a possible teaching position there once my promotion was finalized. NDU is a Department of Defense institution that has a number of schools offering master's degrees for senior military officers and senior civilians in national security. The students tend to be colonels who are likely to become generals, or Foreign Service Officers on track to become ambassadors.

The assignment was a win-win. For me, it was a chance to get back into the classroom, which I love, and use my experiences from Iraq and Afghanistan to prepare the next generation of senior leaders. It was also a way to put some of my doctoral research to good use, since I had been critical of the professional military education system and this was an opportunity to try out some of my recommendations. NDU, meanwhile, would gain a military faculty member with a PhD, which was a rarity. Most of their military faculty held a master's degree, and there had recently been some unpleasant questions in Congress about professors' academic qualifications.

After an interview with the department head and meetings with other faculty members, I was told that I was their choice, and they would make a formal request for me to be assigned there. Colonels' assignments were handled by the Air Force's Senior Leader Management Office, which based most of their decisions on the seniority of the requester. Since the head of NDU was a 3-star admiral, there were not many people who could override her.

~

With my career moving along, I had a chance to think about more running opportunities. When registration opened for the 2009 Marine Corps Marathon, signing up was a no-brainer.

Though I had spent much of the summer training with Ethan again, we were not planning to run together. He had some friends who were running this for the final time that he wanted to join, and I thought I would slow them down, so I headed out on my own. As it turned out, I saw him around the 8-mile point, at the spot by the woods where so many folks stopped to relieve themselves. When I called his name it startled him, and he turned and peed on my leg. Ah, the joys of running marathons.

My friends Linh and Kevin were waiting along the National Mall and again at the Finish Line, so I tried to turn in a good performance. Though I was worried about my potential pace, I managed to cut nearly 14 minutes off my previous personal best. This was the kind of improvement I wanted to see, and I was starting to feel a little cocky about my ability to keep improving.

That cockiness was on full display when I went off to run the Standard Chartered Hong Kong Marathon in February 2010. Because of the nature of my assignment at the Pentagon I had to first get a counterintelligence briefing to make sure I knew who might be watching me and how to avoid having my phone compromised. I told the briefer, "I am there to run a marathon, if the bad guys want to follow me through that they are welcome to try." So, yeah, maybe I was just a bit arrogant.

Unfortunately, this did not end up being one of my better efforts. Since I had done well the previous year I probably came in with unrealistic expectations. What I had forgotten was that in 2009 I had just spent three months living in Singapore, but this time I was coming from Washington DC, where I had been running in snow and freezing temperatures through the winter. Add in the fact that Hong Kong saw its temperature and humidity both shoot up just before I arrived, and I was definitely unprepared for the weather.

I felt fine until the halfway point, but soon after that I started feeling unwell. Just prior to the tunnel going underneath Victoria Harbor I ducked into a port-a-potty and was convinced there was blood in my urine, typically a bad sign (I later realized the sun coming through the orange sides of the toilet was discoloring everything). In any case, I felt like I was dehydrated, and once you feel it, it's a little too late.

My pace slowed dramatically, and I finally took to walking quite a bit. Hong Kong has a rolling time limit, and you have to hit various checkpoints by a certain time or they put you on the bus and send you to the finish area, so I kept very close track of the clock. As it happened, I ducked through the final checkpoint around the 35km mark as they were preparing to close the gate. I managed to push hard during that last stretch, and finally came across the Finish Line about an hour later than I expected.

My local friends Tony and Max were waiting for me – with cupcakes, even – and they were getting scared. They knew when I was planning to arrive but had no way of knowing where I was. Once I recovered my bag I had my phone and called to tell them where to find me. Then I decided to lie down, which was a huge mistake. Everything seized up, and when they found me, I could not move. Max ended up running to get the paramedics, four of whom loaded me carefully into a wheelchair and led me to the medical tent.

Tony stayed with me while they checked me out, and except for low blood pressure and dehydration, I was not that bad. There were people being loaded into ambulances, and I told the doctor, "Please don't send me to the hospital; I have a flight in a few hours." That might not be the smartest thing that I have ever said, but fortunately, there was nothing seriously wrong with me.

I left Hong Kong with a much better appreciation for my own limits and a realization that I could not expect to just automatically be faster in each race. I took that attitude to Cincinnati in May, when Ethan and I flew off to run the Flying Pig Marathon. Ethan has a large collection of pigs in different forms, and when he saw the medal he said, "I want that. Let's go run the marathon." It's as good a reason as any, I suppose.

This was not the first time we had travelled together, but it was the first time it was just the two of us, and I learned that Ethan is a great travel partner. The whole trip was very relaxed as he refuses to get stressed about anything, and frankly that offers a nice contrast to me, as I tend to get very detail-oriented.

He is also a great running partner, and after the Hong Kong experience I had decided I just wanted to run with him without worrying about timing. The day started off wet, as a pre-dawn thunderstorm poured down on us while we were walking to the Starting Line. A brief power outage knocked out the lights and the PA system, and we worried they would call off the race, but things cleared to a drizzle and off we went.

The Flying Pig is a fun race that winds through downtown as well as going through some residential neighborhoods. Rather than getting upset about the traffic disruption, the residents turn out to see which neighborhood can put on the best support for the runners. Though there was rain coming down throughout most of the race, and Ethan's leg started giving him problems about a few miles from the end, we still had a great time. As we neared the Finish Line and Ethan was in pain, I tried to push him along, yelling "Come on, come on, we're almost there, we're going to do this, we're going to get pig medals, let's go, let's go," until he finally yelled "Will, shut up!" and I realized he did not really need any more encouragement.

~

It was around this time that my professional life took an unexpected turn: I decided to retire from the Air Force.

That spring, when assignments for the next year were announced, things did not go as planned. Despite the policy that the most senior person requesting you will get you, I learned there was an exception: going to Iraq or Afghanistan took priority. Rather than sending me to National Defense University, the Air Force instead decided to send me to a one-year position in Baghdad, into a role that was very similar to what I had done there five years earlier as a much more junior officer.

If I took the assignment, I would go into a position where they seemed to just be looking for someone with a pulse and an eagle insignia on his collar, whereas the NDU position needed someone with my unique background. Following the year in Baghdad, there was no telling where I would be posted for my next assignment, so I was looking at the possibility of spending the next three years wasting my talents. On the other hand, if I turned down the assignment, I would also be turning down the promotion and be forced to retire within two months. After grappling with the decision for a week, I realized what was most important to me, and elected to retire.

Even though being a colonel had never been a goal of mine, this was still a depressing time. Despite the fact that my PhD focused on organizational change, I have always been much more comfortable studying the changes happening to others than I have been with experiencing sudden changes myself. Add in the fact that for my entire life I had either been a military brat or a military officer, and this represented a disruption of everything I had ever known.

My job search started right away, and turned out better than expected. The master's degree program in human resource management at Georgetown University was hunting for a Visiting Professor, and after a few months of waiting for email replies, I got the position just a week before classes started. I really felt like I had landed on my feet, going from being depressed over the sudden change in my life, to being on the faculty of one of the best universities in the United States.

One advantage of teaching is that it affords some flexibility, which proved useful once I decided to run the New York City Marathon that November. I had not made it in though the lottery, so instead I signed up to run for a charity known as Fred's Team, which supports the Memorial Sloan-Kettering Cancer Center. Even though I had not raised money for anything in a long time, I found this to be an exceptionally rewarding experience, and I enjoyed the chance to meet up with other Fred's Team runners in New York.

Ethan accompanied me there, as did my friends Adrian and Shawn. After all, who says "no" to a weekend in New York? While they went out Friday and Saturday nights, I stayed in and took it easy, and was also careful not to be walking around too much on Saturday. We went out Saturday night for a pasta dinner, then I was up early Sunday morning to meet the hundreds of other Fred's Team runners and take the bus to the Starting Line on Staten Island.

The New York City Marathon will always be one of my favorite races. As if the iconic nature of the start across the Verrazano Narrows Bridge was not enough, we were cheered by huge crowds all the way to the Finish Line. My greatest memory is coming across the Queensboro Bridge into Manhattan and hearing a strange roar, like the sound of industrial air conditioners atop a high rise. That seemed odd, since it was November, but as we made the turn onto First Avenue, I realized what it was: tens of thousands of people along both sides of the street, going absolutely crazy as we ran north. I tried to find my friends but there was no way that was happening in that crowd.

During the final few miles along Fifth Avenue I knew I was not going to break the four-hour mark, but was still going strong despite some pain that had started earlier as I ran through the Bronx. Once I got into Central Park, I finally saw my friends, and slowed just a bit so Adrian could get some good photos. Then it was time for a final push through Columbus Circle and back to the Finish Line, coming in at 4:07:52, a new personal best.

2010 had been a strange year, good in many ways but with some unexpected twists. It started on my birthday in January with me setting my goal of running the Marathon Grand Slam, then turned sharply when I decided to retire, before moving onto an interesting route with my appointment to the Georgetown faculty. Along the way I had a not-so-great race in Hong Kong, a fun race with Ethan at the Flying Pig, and an amazing time in New York. None of those, however, moved me any closer to the Grand Slam. It was time to go to Paris.

~

The next April, I took full advantage of the flexibility of my teaching role, flying out Wednesday night with plans to return the following Monday before my next class. Ethan and I took different flights because we were each collecting miles in different airline frequent-flyer programs, but we landed at about the same time and met up at baggage claim. We took the train into the city and got set up at our hotel, which was close to the starting area. This was the point where I started realizing the importance of hotel loyalty programs since, based on my status, we were upgraded to a larger room, and we had breakfast each day and other amenities. I was not quite feeling like George Clooney's frequent traveler in *Up in the Air*, but I was getting close.

This was Ethan's first visit to Paris, and only my third, so we had a lot to see. We tried to be careful not to walk around so much that we wore ourselves out, but the weather was so nice that it was easy to stay out for the whole day. We unfortunately misjudged the Paris Metro closing time, though, and Thursday night found us stuck a few miles from our hotel with a shortage of taxis nearby. We ended up finding what looked like a Thai tuk-tuk that had a loose connection in the battery and kept dying, but we finally made it back to the hotel after about an hour of sputtering along.

We did all the things one should do in Paris, including the Louvre, the Eiffel Tower, and of course checking out the nightlife. Getting there a few days before the race allowed us to explore without trying to do it all the day before the race and wearing ourselves out in the process. We also took a little time for ourselves, which I have usually found is a good idea when traveling with friends. We can each do our own thing for a few hours and then we have stories to share. Ethan had a relative in the city that he was connecting with, and I popped into a shop to find a birthday present for a friend. All in all, we had a nice walk around town before it was time to run around town.

~

Finally, it was race day. The weather was beautiful: a nice cool morning, with a trace of clouds that offered some coverage from the sun but without a threat of rain. If anything, it was a little bit too cool, but we knew it would heat up soon enough. Still, when we went out we fashioned a couple plastic garbage bags into ponchos, something we could discard as we got started.

Ethan made the choice to wear tights, something I didn't think was especially necessary. I only wore tights during winter training and had never yet been in a race where I thought they made sense. His metabolism is different from mine, though, and he tends not to warm up as easily, so he thought they would be a good idea. That's one reason it is hard to ask for advice sometimes; everyone is a bit different, with different requirements.

When we registered we put ourselves into different timing brackets. I was aiming to improve my personal best, while Ethan was planning to run a time similar to our Flying Pig experience. The Paris Marathon was big enough that they used corrals based on expected timing, so he would line up a few thousand people behind me. That being the case, we waited until the last minute to make our way to our particular starting areas.

Our stretching took place outside the Louis Vuitton flagship store, and it was nice to have gotten there with enough time that we didn't have to worry about rushing around. All too often we are fighting our way through the public transit, but in this case our hotel was just a short walk away. We had time to get the blood moving and feel comfortably warmed up. This may be one reason for the success we would have later that day.

I got into my corral and the waiting began. One of the first things I noticed was the diversity of languages around me. My only overseas races to this point had been in Singapore and Hong Kong, so I was used to being surrounded by Chinese speakers. This time, though, I heard

French, Russian, German, Spanish, Italian, and a bit of English with various accents thrown in for good measure.

The gun went off at 8:45am and we started moving slowly forward. Once we crossed the line the road actually opened up a bit, not only as people started running, but also as quite a few ducked off into the trees along the right side of the road to get rid of the excess water they had drunk while waiting for the start. There are a few trees off to the side, but they did not offer much in the way of privacy.

The first couple of miles were a little frustrating as the road was not exactly an open route. There were concrete medians in the street and I found myself jumping up onto them and having to watch my step as the crowd flowed through a road that suddenly seemed narrower that it did when we had walked along it the previous couple of days. Some people bounced up onto the sidewalks to escape the mass in the street.

Our first few miles took us through neighborhoods that Ethan and I had explored, and that familiarity always makes things easier for me. We ran down Rue di Rivoli, and I started realizing what a great visual spectacle this race was likely to be. The architecture of Paris is wonderful, and this was my first time experiencing it early in the morning. As we passed the Bastille I tried to take it all in while staying focused on not running into people.

That became tricky a bit later. A right turn up near Chateau de Vincennes was a bit sharper than was good for the race, and it turned into a bottleneck. I felt myself slowing almost to a walk as we tried to navigate the turn in a large mass of people. I started getting upset with the race organizers for putting such a turn at this point. We were a quarter of the way through the race and this was not the time that most runners would want their pace disrupted like that. Looking back on it later I realized there are a lot of limits involved in laying out a course, and maybe before complaining I should learn what goes into it. At the time, though, it bugged me a lot.

We spent about 6 miles in the park, and contrary to my expectations, there were quite a few spectators out there. This was nothing like the New York City crowd, of course. There was no mass transit available in the park, nor was there parking for cars, but Parisians are a little more used to riding bikes and scooters than we are in the US, so it was easy enough to get out there. I saw a number of local running groups cheering on their members, in addition to lots of signs for individual friends and family members. Everyone was cheering in French, of course, so I could not be sure exactly what they were yelling, but the sentiment was clear.

Coming out of the park we were parallel to our earlier route but closer to the Siene, and after about 3 miles we took a little turn that put us right along the river. It was starting to get a bit hot by this point. Our path took us downhill and underneath a bridge, and I wanted to just stay in the shade as long as I could rather than slogging back uphill and out into the sun again.

By this point we were past the halfway mark and I was watching my time carefully. After training hard through the winter and into the spring, I saw this as a great chance to finally break my 4-hour barrier. I had planned where I should be by different times, and so far I was on track for a strong finish.

At the same time, I was really taken by the whole experience. Soon after we passed the 18-mile point, when I was concerned about hitting the wall soon, I looked to my left and saw the Eiffel Tower climbing up just across the river. I thought to myself, "When am I ever going to run past the Eiffel Tower again?," and though I did not quite surrender to the moment and just focus on my surroundings, it did make me wonder about the experiences I would have and the places I would see on my Grand Slam journey. There is something to be said for just being in the moment and not worrying about what your watch says, and that glance across the river was a good reminder.

Of course, nothing says you cannot enjoy the experience while also running fast, so I kept trying to push myself. I felt like I was slowing down a little bit, but it was not too dramatic. I was definitely feeling the effects of the miles, but not to the point of exhaustion. At this point, I felt like I was regulating my body pretty well.

As we moved into a residential area I noticed something unique: the French did not clear their parked cars off the street. In every race before, the city had ordered cars off of the streets and into driveways or parking lots, giving us plenty of room to spread out. The French, however, chose not to worry about such things. In my mind's eye I could see a local official telling residents they would need to move their cars, and a beret-wearing man with a thin mustache and smoking a cigarette yelling back while waving his hands in the air. A stereotype, yes, but at that point my mind was focused more on the pain in my legs than on being culturally respectful.

Continuing on, I realized the density of the neighborhood probably did not leave many places to put a car other than on the street, so I just navigated around them and blocked it out of my mind. We control what we can, and we do not worry about the rest – that seems like a good philosophy, anyway. I was realizing that, whereas American cities may have been designed with cars – or at least, horses and buggies – in mind, Paris had been around a lot longer, and concepts of urban planning were not quite the same back then. It reinforced the point that running marathons through cities would let me observe things I might not notice as a normal tourist.

Most of the final 6 miles were spent winding our way through another park. Upon entering it we looped around the tennis stadiums at Roland Garros, where the French Open is played. I had watched the Open many times on TV and had toured Roland Garros a few years earlier, but as we passed them I had the thought that, "well, now I'm an athlete too." That was probably the first time I ever thought of myself that way, but I felt like I was as much a part of this race as any tennis player was a part of the Open.

It was approaching noon by this point, and it was starting to feel pretty hot; I developed a new appreciation for the earlier start times in Asia. Keeping an eye on my watch, I knew I was falling behind the pace I needed for a sub-4 finish, and try as I might I did not seem to be able to pick up the speed. I was not to the point of walking, I was passing plenty of people, and I was able to hold a pretty steady pace, but it was too slow to hit my goal. Doing the math in my head, I could not see a way to make it happen, and a self-defeating sense of depression hit. I get the feeling that once your brain says, "it cannot happen," your body accepts it and ensures that it doesn't.

Still, I was moving along at a pace that could get me to a new personal best, so I didn't give up. My brain, though, was not done playing tricks on me. Ethan and I had not checked out the Finish Line, and in my mind I was thinking it was at the Arc de Triomphe. In reality, though, it was on the road leading to the roundabout. When I saw the arch in the distance it fooled my brain into thinking I still had quite a distance to go, the kilometer markers along the road notwithstanding. As the crowd multiplied, though, I realized I was in the home stretch, and really kicked it in to finish strong.

Stepping across the Finish Line I hit the stop button on my watch and looked a moment later: 4:05:57. Not breaking the 4-hour barrier, but still a new personal best, and something I could be very happy about. I collected my medal and walked through the Finish Line festival area for a bit to clear my head, but I had some unfinished business: Ethan was still out there.

Since we had not scoped out the area in advance I was not immediately sure how to get back to where all the spectators had been when I was approaching the Finish Line. I knew I wanted to get back there quickly, since Ethan was probably not more than about 20 or 30 minutes behind me. Finally, I just ducked between two booths and under a rope and got into the crowd of folks still moving back toward the cheering section.

I reached a point about 200 meters from the Finish Line and waited. The tough thing about standing there was that I had no way of knowing if he had already gone past, and if I missed him in the crowded field of runners, I would not know it for a while. I figured I would wait half an hour, and then make my way to the meeting point we had picked out near the arch.

Fortunately, he came along a few minutes later, and he was easy to spot. There were not that many runners wearing black tights and a red top, nor were there that many Vietnamese men, so he stood out in the crowd. I yelled his name but he was very focused on just reaching the Finish Line. I managed to snap a photo of him, and then headed for our meeting point. Naturally, we had managed to confuse each other, and we each ended up waiting at different places. After about half an hour I walked back to the hotel, and he was already there.

The important thing, of course, is that we both finished, and I had taken my first big step since deciding to pursue the Grand Slam.

~ 6 ~
South America
Rio de Janeiro Marathon
Rio de Janeiro, Brazil
July 17, 2011

Once I was back from Paris it was time to start making some big decisions.

I had really been enjoying my teaching experience at Georgetown, especially during the first semester. The primary course they assigned me was not something I was keen to teach: Data Analysis for HR. I am not the strongest statistician in the world, and I felt like my PhD and my professional experience made me more suitable for some of the other courses in the curriculum, but by the time they officially hired me, this was the course that absolutely needed a professor.

A required course for the HR management master's degree, it was something everyone had to take, but it also made many people very nervous. During the previous year the class had two adjunct professors team-teaching it; both were data specialists, and from what I could see in their syllabus, they taught it largely as a statistics course. The short time that I had between getting hired and starting classes meant I could not select another book – the university bookstore had already stocked the text from last year's class – but at least I could change the syllabus.

My goal for the course was not for the students to learn everything they could about statistical methods, but instead, for them to learn how to frame questions, figure out what information they needed, find that information, and use it to make an informed decision. They did not have to be statisticians, but they needed to be able to understand what the statisticians were telling them. I was determined to make this more of a business course than a math class, but the book did not help.

I was a bit stressed by the short timeframe in which to get ready but, once classes started in September 2010, I was so happy to be back in the classroom. The first night we met, Beyoncé was playing a concert downtown. I told the students I was sorry to make them miss it, and when we went around the room to do introductions I asked for their name, their undergraduate background, their professional experience, and their favorite Beyoncé song. "Single Ladies" was #1 by far. If they remembered nothing else after the semester, many did seem to remember that.

As much as I enjoyed those first few months, that probably was not my best semester as a teacher. I had trouble leading the students away from the emphasis on the math and lifting them up to a broader business focus. That was my fault, not theirs; I just hadn't figured out the best way to teach this course yet.

Case in point: I handed out a short project mid-semester, along with some data sets they could use. A couple days later, one student called me almost in tears, saying, "I'm digging through all the data and I can't find any patterns, I don't see any trends, I just don't know what to do!!" I tried to calm him down, telling him, "It's okay, it's okay, just start with this: what question are you trying to answer?" "Well," he replied, "I have not gotten that far yet." Considering that knowing what you're trying to figure out would normally be the first step, I suddenly discovered what his problem was. It was a sign that I needed to work harder to get them to the goals I had set for the semester.

Among the nice surprises about the class was that I had some marathoners in there, including some who had run Boston. I tried to soak up whatever lessons I could get from them, picking up some tips I could use as I prepared for New York, then Paris, then Rio. One of the greatest things about teaching is how much you can learn from your students, so in that sense this semester was definitely a success.

That first semester may have started off very stressfully, but I had a wonderful time with those students. Years later I am still in touch with quite a few of them, and have exchanged professional advice with many of them, which has hopefully helped them but which has certainly helped me in my work.

As much fun as it was, though, a new opportunity was about to pop up that would require some important choices.

~

Over New Year's I decided to go back to Singapore for the holiday. I had visited there briefly a few months after returning home from the Fulbright, and had met up with some of my friends as we happened to be in cities at the same time, but this would be a more extended visit. I was also taking the opportunity to visit Angkor Wat in Cambodia for a few days, something I had not done before.

I ended up bringing quite a bit of work with me. I had graded all my final exams before Christmas and ensured all the grades were turned in, but I was also part of the Capstone course, and that still needed to be finished. Capstone was essentially the master's thesis for the program, and I was one of two professors involved in it. The adjunct professor who led the course conducted some "how to" research classes, while I advised half the students on their paper and she took the other half. I had a stack of papers with me on the trip, and I settled in and worked on some each day.

An interesting aspect of the grading was that, per the program dean's instructions, the adjunct and I traded students when it came to the final paper. I graded those students whom she had been advising, while she graded mine. I thought this was a little odd; after all, the best person to know if my students have met the expectations we agreed on is me, and the same should go for her. What we were doing now was similar to me giving my students an exam, and another professor grading them. I raised this point to the head of the program but, not for the first time, I was told "that's just how we do it here."

In addition to my courses, I had also been serving as the academic advisor for the hundred or so students in the program. This basically meant helping them choose classes, handling the paperwork for transfer credits, and helping those with challenging situations try to work through them. Fortunately, all those details had been settled before my trip, and I didn't expect students to start calling with problems until a few days before classes started, so I didn't have to worry too much about that part of the job.

Though I got my papers graded, I certainly didn't spend all my vacation working, but instead spent most of it catching up with friends over the holidays. At dinner one night, a fellow who worked for a local non-profit was complaining about their executive director, and we talked through some of the challenges in their working environment and what they might do about it. He then mentioned that the director was planning to leave in 2011 and, he said, "You should apply for the job."

I didn't say much more about it that night, but I thought about it a lot every day afterwards. Move to Singapore? The idea had always been there in the back of my mind. One of the reasons for doing the Fulbright in the first place had been to "test drive" the country, giving me a chance to see what it was like to live there without committing myself to it for the long term. I had enjoyed it my first time around, so should I consider it further?

Over the next few days, a similar theme kept popping up among my friends: "We thought you were coming back after you retired from the Air Force, so why haven't you?" Good question. The possibility had occurred to me when I was retiring, but with all the changes already going on in such a short period, I did not think that searching for a job overseas, and then packing up and moving around the world, was what I needed to be doing.

Coming back to the US, I talked about it with Linh and he suggested I should go for it. Singapore is a good place to live, I already had friends there, and it's a great jumping-off point for exploring the rest of Asia. I was enjoying teaching at Georgetown, but certainly there were enjoyable jobs in Singapore, too. If I could find a good role – I wasn't sure I was the best pick to lead this particular non-profit, so I should look for something else – then maybe I should give it a try.

I considered how such a move would fit into my Grand Slam plans. With Europe scheduled for April, and South America planned for July, there would be four locations I still needed to do. Being in Southeast Asia would put me closer to Australia, and could make Africa more accessible, depending on which country I chose. The North Pole and Antarctica would be a little farther, but it was a hurdle I could easily overcome. I also figured that running in Singapore's hot climate would toughen me up and make me faster when I went elsewhere, much like training at high altitude helps you be stronger and faster when you race closer to sea level.

With all my information in hand, I decided to at least start exploring job opportunities. My plan was to focus on teaching positions first, with consulting as a second option, in-house HR as a third, and, finally, general management. As Ethan and I prepared for Paris, I began applying to universities and firms.

Once we were back from Paris, I started getting very close to a decision point. Georgetown needed to know if I planned to return the following year. My contract as a Visiting Professor was written on an annual basis, and they had already let me know they wanted me to stay. As the end of April approached, I was going to have to make a choice, because if I said I would stay then I was committed to being there through the next academic year.

As I returned from Paris, a friend who worked for a consulting firm mentioned that their Singapore office was expanding and they needed a consultant who could work with senior HR leaders. I had actually had an interview with the firm the previous year for a research position in Washington DC, but this would instead be an advisory role working directly with clients. He knew the head of the Singapore office very well and offered to send her my resume.

The response was quick, and very positive. I soon had a phone call with the managing director in Singapore, and though there was certainly no job offer yet, there was a commitment to some additional interviews. For me, though, it was decision time, as Georgetown needed to know my plans.

On the one hand, I was really enjoying being back in the classroom and working with so many great students. On the other hand, I was excited about the thought of living overseas. Plus, I knew my role at Georgetown was about change, as my program dean wanted me to take on a lot of his administrative duties in the coming year. The biggest risk, of course, was that I didn't actually have a job, and would be giving up my current paycheck in the hopes that something else was going to work out.

One of the things that distance running has done for me is help me to take the long view of things. During a race, I can push through a hilly patch when I know there is flat terrain ahead. Rather than just thinking about the next step, I think about the next ten miles. As I pursued the Grand Slam, I was looking ahead to races that would not take place for a few more years. All of that has helped me look beyond what is happening now to what is possible in the future.

With all of this in mind, I rolled the dice, told Georgetown I would not be returning after teaching the summer semester, and went to Rio knowing my job would end soon after returning.

~

The trip from Washington DC to Rio was easy enough, though of course it was pretty long. During my flight to Houston, where I would change planes, the fellow next to me asked me about my plans. As I told him I was flying down to run the marathon he got all excited and was telling his friend, "This guy's going to Rio to run a marathon!" Even later, walking through the Houston airport, I heard him point me out to

86

another friend as "that's the guy going to Brazil to race in a marathon." For a brief moment, I felt like a very, very, very, very minor celebrity.

Arriving in Rio, I quickly settled into my temporary neighborhood. I was staying in Copacabana, a couple blocks from some of Rio's, and the world's, most beautiful beaches. Though it was winter according to the calendar, Rio's location gives it great weather during that time of year, and the beaches were full.

I was a little careful taking advantage of the beaches. I love laying out on a beach and having a drink with a little umbrella just as much as the next guy, but I also knew that running a marathon while sunburned would not be fun. I had planned the trip so I would have a couple days there after the race, so I decided to explore the city now and relax later.

Copacabana and nearby Ipanema were easy enough to navigate. The subway stations scattered about made it easy to maneuver between different parts of town, and were great for avoiding the traffic when I made my way to the runners' expo. The whole city had a great energy to it; there seemed to be a celebration of some sort going on no matter where I went, whether some kind of festival or simply marking someone's birthday. The people I chatted with, whether running a food stall, working in a shop, or just riding on the subway, all seemed to be smiling.

Every travel guide I had read suggested being careful in Rio, especially down close to the beaches where the developed area bumps up against the favelas. While I always try to see the best in everyone, I was staying very aware of my surroundings. I only had a couple of tense moments, once when two people seemed to be following me, and another time when a drunk man approached me on the sidewalk and started pushing me and screaming at me. Both of those situations got resolved pretty quickly, though.

While I wanted to see "normal life" in the city, I also wanted to visit the Christ the Redeemer statue on Mount Corcovado, which I realize is a very touristy thing to do. It's a global icon, of course, and certainly something I wanted to see. When Linh and I had been in Lisbon the previous year I had seen the taller Christ the King statue from a distance, but now I wanted to get up close and personal. After figuring out the bus system and finding the tram up the mountain, I found the experience was definitely worth it. While the statue itself is very impressive, the view from the top of the mountain is simply unbelievable, and any visitors to Rio who don't experience it are shortchanging themselves.

~

Finally, it was race day. As the morning began, I quickly imagined myself simply playing a role in a comedy set in Brazil. Michael Caine once starred in a movie called *Blame it on Rio* and that pretty much describes my attitude for the pre- and post-race period.

Since the race was point-to-point, rather than an out-and-back route or a circle, the Starting Line was nearly 40 kilometers from my hotel. The marathon had arranged for shuttle buses to get us to the Starting Line, and those were relatively close to my hotel but still a required a taxi rather than being in walking distance. The buses were near the Finish Line, and so the roads around there would soon be closed to most traffic, owing to the race that would be starting in a few hours.

Let me pause for a moment and offer a quick lesson learned: if you are in a foreign country and taking a taxi to a place that may require some explanation, find a hotel employee who speaks your language, describe to them where you are going, and then ask them to tell the taxi driver. As you can guess, that's pretty much the opposite of what I did.

I waited outside for a while; there were not very many taxis driving around before sunrise. A couple of hotel staff, including what appeared to be a doorman, were hanging around outside but didn't seem to have any interest in helping me. I finally walked over to a bigger street and managed to find a cab there. I was carrying a map showing where the shuttle buses would be, but the driver was either unable to read the map or simply uninterested.

As we approached the park where the Finish Line would be and where the shuttle buses were supposed to be parked, we started running into road closures. At least, I think that's what was happening. All I knew for sure is that the driver was yelling at me in Portuguese and waving his arms, and my reply of "No falo portugues" did nothing to deter him.

Finally, he pulled to the side of the road, looked back to me, and very slowly and loudly repeated what he had been saying. It took all my self-control not to laugh. A common stereotype of Americans is that, when we find ourselves talking to someone who does not speak English, we just speak more slowly and more loudly, since obviously they will understand us then. It was pretty funny being on the receiving end of it.

We drove a bit farther and suddenly, on the other side of the park, I saw a line of buses. I got him to stop, managed to figure out the fare, and bounced out of the cab and across the grass to the waiting shuttles. I tried to ask someone if these were the buses to the Starting Line, but only got a blank look, until I pulled out my bus reservation sheet that was in Portuguese, and suddenly got smiles and was pointed onto the proper bus.

If it seems like I am critical of Brazilians, or anyone else, for not understanding my English, let me be clear: I am not. When I go to another country and have trouble getting around because I don't speak the language, that's my fault, no one else's. It is up to me to figure out how to get around; it is not up to another country to learn my language just to accommodate me. As a consultant I certainly understand the value of using English as a language for business, even among countries for whom English is not a first language – in the ASEAN Economic Community, for instance, the common business language is English – but for me to expect taxi drivers and shop clerks in Brazil to speak English would be ridiculous.

There were buses leaving every 15 minutes, so I found the 5:15am bus for which I had made my reservation, and settled in for a ride. There were plenty of buses after mine, but I thought it was more important to make sure I got to the Starting Line on time than it was to get an extra 15 or 30 minutes of sleep.

That turned out to be a pretty smart move. As we drove I was chatting with my seatmate, who had come from Sao Paulo. We talked about Rio winning their bids for the 2014 World Cup and the 2016 Olympics, and he was telling me about all the construction going on. As we talked, I suddenly noticed the bus slowing and the sound of the engine diminishing. We pulled off to the side of the road and came to a dead stop. "Ah, Brazil," said the fellow next to me.

Ah, Brazil, indeed. We waited for a few minutes with no word on what had happened. Finally, the driver walked back and started passing the news. The Brazilian runner next to me just chuckled and shook his head, but I still had no idea what had happened. He turned to me and with a sigh said, "We ran out of gas."

Fortunately, another bus had left 15 minutes after us. Unfortunately, it was full, but this was Brazil, where the answer to the question "how many people can fit on a bus?" is always, "a few more." When the next bus came along it stopped, we filed on, and stood in close quarters in the aisle as the bus bucked and swayed along the way to the Starting Line.

Once we arrived at the starting area, everything seemed pretty well organized. There were drinks and food, and we had plenty of space to stretch and get warmed up. The sun was just starting to rise, and as we were along a beach on the eastern side of the country, the view of the sun rising up from the ocean was gorgeous. I knew that in a little while I was really going to hate the sun overhead, but for now it was beautiful.

Every 15 minutes another shuttle brought a busload of runners, and it seemed like no one else had run out of gas. As the area started filling up, a guy sitting next to me asked if I was American. Looking forward to chatting with a local runner I replied that I was, only to find that so was he. In fact, his home was about 20 miles from mine outside Washington DC, though he was spending a year in Brazil as an English teacher.

All of the announcements were in Portuguese, so I just followed other runners as race time approached. We moved into the starting corrals and waited for the gun. The race also served as the marathon for the Military World Games that were taking place in Rio that week, so those runners moved to the front along with all the other elites. They took off, and the rest of us awaited our turn.

Once that turn came, we were off. It felt like a great day for a race. The temperature was cool, with fairly low humidity, and there was no wind. The skies were clear, so there was no chance of rain, though unfortunately that also meant no cover from the sun as it climbed higher.

Most of the race was run along the beach, which for about 30 kilometers would be pretty isolated. This was not a tourist-oriented stretch of beach, but instead seemed to be an area where rich people who could afford to live privately would buy a house. The homes were to the left side of the road, many of them hidden behind walls, while the beach was to our right.

The road was closed, of course, so no one drove out to watch us. Few of the people living in the homes along the way seemed interested in the runners passing by, so we didn't see many of them. Most of the spectators tended to be the volunteers along the way or the few hardy souls who had ridden their bikes to watch for friends. It felt a bit like running through Singapore in terms of the crowd, though the weather was definitely much nicer for running.

Along the way there were a few runners having trouble. There seemed to be quite a few people falling out with twisted ankles or cramps. At one point, a lady had collapsed and appeared to be having a seizure. In all cases, fortunately, they seemed to have friends with them, and in the case of the lady with the seizure it appeared that some runners with medical training had stopped to help. Runners are certainly good about helping others.

From my perspective, the race was pretty peaceful. I was excited to be there, and was enjoying the experience. Running along the ocean offered one of the best race routes I had enjoyed so far, the weather was very nice, my body felt fine, and it was just a good day overall.

I had started this race with an uncertain goal. Having set a personal best in Paris and coming so close to the 4-hour mark, I thought this could be a chance to push just a little harder and finally break through that barrier that had been haunting me. My preparation in the three months in between, though, had not been as intense as my pre-Paris training, and I felt like just enjoying the run. Ultimately, I decided to just go out strong and see what would happen. That might not be the best way to run in a particular time, but it was a good way to enjoy the day.

For the first half I felt very good. My pace was excellent, I was hydrating well, and I wasn't feeling any unexpected pain. As we moved toward the residential and tourist areas of Leblon, Ipanema, and Copacabana, we encountered a hill and it seemed to hit me hard. I had been running more or less equally with two guys from Poland; we kept passing one another but stayed in sight of each other. As we got near the top of the hill, however, they moved past me and I could not find the energy to catch them.

This left me frustrated, and I started telling myself, "This is ridiculous, you are so out of shape, you cannot even run up a stupid hill." After a couple kilometers of beating myself up, I thought, "Well, then again, you ARE running a marathon." If you stop and think about it, the very fact I was running a marathon suggested I was probably in pretty good shape. It was a sign of how high my standards had risen. Three years earlier I had never run a marathon, and now I was berating myself for not running one fast enough. Times had certainly changed.

As we moved into Leblon we started seeing more people along the road, especially when we were closest to the beach. At this point everyone was mostly local, as we had not quite hit the tourist areas yet. Coming down the hill and sliding into Ipanema put us into a bigger, and more international, crowd.

The roads were still closed, of course, but plenty of people were out on foot. Many of them seemed confused by all the runners going by, unsure about what we were running from or what we were running toward. There were a few cheers from people who realized what we were doing, but even they were mostly just waiting to get across the road in between us.

Transitioning into Copacabana, we were now in familiar territory where I had been spending most of my time. The beach was a bit more crowded than in the days before since the locals had Sunday off, and there were more people lining the road. As we approached the 38km point, there would be a left turn that would carry us away from the beaches and toward the Finish Line. Since this turn was about two blocks from my hotel, I had been walking past it for the past few days, and my anticipation grew as I recognized that it was coming soon.

The crowd was big at the turn, probably because this was a major intersection. We also had more people along the route from here on out. Traveling companions who had come with runners, local friends and families cheering someone on, and casual passers-by all lined the road as we turned inland.

One marketing point for the race was that we would be running toward the Christ the Redeemer statue toward the end. That was sort of true. We could certainly see the statue in the distance atop Mount Corcovado to our left, but it's not like it was a key feature in our field of view. Still, though, much as I had enjoyed running past the Eiffel Tower in Paris, I thought it was fun to be running with this iconic landmark in front of me.

Though it was winter in Brazil, the temperature was definitely climbing as we moved through the final few kilometers. It was still much cooler than it would be back in Washington DC on this day, but we had a cloudless sky, and as the sun climbed higher it seemed to be beating down stronger and stronger. Plenty of people were walking by this point, but I was determined not to, and so far I had stuck to that.

Pounding toward the Finish Line, I could see the colorful tents approaching on my left, with the sun bouncing off the water to my right. Finally, I saw the banner over the street marking the Finish, and as I passed the 42km marker I went all out for the final steps. Realizing that I still had the energy for a strong push at the end made me a little mad later, since that meant I probably could have been pushing harder in the second half of the race, but at the moment I didn't really care. I crossed the line at 4:20:45, not as fast as at Paris, but at that point I was a very happy man.

Walking into the finish area with my medal around my neck, I heard music playing somewhere nearby. Actually, I always heard music playing no matter where I was in Rio, but this sounded like a national anthem. Sure enough, the podium was nearby and the winners were receiving their awards and their big novelty checks. I looked a bit longingly at the podium, thinking it would be nice to end up there someday, but then I returned to the goals I had already established. I looked forward to having the Grand Slam medal around my neck, and if there were no crowds or podiums or big novelty checks, that would be fine.

Making my way through the rest of the area, I found plenty of food and athletic retailers, and a party atmosphere that was a bit more muted that normal for Rio, probably because everyone had just been running for a few hours. I stumbled across a tent with a banner reading "International Athletes" and I decided, "Hey, I'm an international athlete," so I stopped in to hang out with other foreigners and get something to eat. I think it was actually a tent for some of the elites and invited runners, but I decided to let myself feel special for just a little while.

When the time came to go back to the hotel, I realized the transportation gods were not done with me. As if my earlier taxi and bus experiences were not enough, I was now unable to find a taxi stand, or any place at all where taxis were stopping. Getting back to the hotel was starting to become a challenge.

I had printed a map showing how to get to the nearest subway station, and I could take the train to get close to the hotel and into an area I recognized, but first I had to find the station. Whether I was reading the map upside down, or simply didn't understand the Portuguese directions, I'll never know, but I think I walked in the opposite direction of the station. After more than an hour, I finally found it, and made my way back.

A year and a half after setting my Grand Slam goal, I was now done with four continents. I was halfway there, but life was about to change again, and my progress was about to slow down.

~ 7 ~
Africa
Cape Town Marathon
Cape Town, South Africa
September 23, 2012

I went for a very long stretch without running a marathon, something I would prefer not to do again.

When I returned from Rio I only had a couple weeks left of the summer semester course I was teaching, and then my time at Georgetown would be over. The summer had been a lot of fun, as I got to teach a new course, Multinational Business Policy and Geopolitics, which might not sound exciting to a lot of people but which fit well with everything I had studied and had done in my career so far. It was a great few months.

My interviews with the consulting company were moving along, which was good since I was not getting a lot of interest from other companies or universities in Singapore. I had spent a couple hours in a phone interview with the head of the Asia-Pacific region, who said he would recommend they hire me, and had in-person interviews with two of the senior people in the department where I would be working. I knew from the interviews that the position was new and the work was currently being handled by other people in the office, so if they wanted to hire me I assumed everything would happen pretty fast once they did.

Trouble popped up at the end of July, just as the last Georgetown paycheck was about to arrive. I had an email from someone at the company saying she hoped I would be accepting their offer, but it was not the HR person. When I wrote back and asked, "Do you know something I don't?" I was told that I should check with the HR specialist with whom I had been talking. She was on vacation, so it was a couple days before I got a reply.

The reply was not what I expected. In the two days between the initial confusion about whether I was hired and the time I got in contact with HR, the company had implemented a global hiring freeze. Three months earlier, Standard & Poor had downgraded its rating for US government securities and scared the global economy, and the trickle down effect had finally reached me. Concerned about costs, the company froze all new hires while they evaluated their positions around the world to see what was really needed.

The result was that, not only was I not hired, they could not even tell me officially if there was an offer. If they had contacted me sooner instead of worrying about telling other people in the company first, I could have at least seen the details so I could evaluate the offer and decide if it was acceptable. Now, though, even though they were hinting that there was an offer waiting for me, they could not tell me anything about it. The plan was for the freeze to be in place until the start of September, and everything should be fine after that.

August came and went, and as we got into September there was no movement. I was doing a little freelance consulting work, but I didn't really have much going on. Finally, in a fit of optimism, I registered for the Standard Chartered Marathon in Singapore that December. I figured that either they will have hired me and I'll be living there, or I will be starting in 2012 but need to go look for an apartment, or if nothing else I can just go and enjoy the race. As it turned out, the second possibility is what happened.

On Halloween I officially got the offer, and while the salary was a little lower than I hoped for, it was still in the range I was considering. It didn't take me long to say yes, and we agreed on a January start date.

That meant I needed an apartment, so my trip to run the marathon would work out well. I arrived in Singapore the week before the race, met with the folks in my new office, and started searching for a place to live. Since I had been unemployed since July and was getting close to the end of my emergency savings, I stayed in a hotel that I only later realized was kind of a "hot sheets" place. As I left around 3:30am to go to the Starting Line, I saw couples just coming in, apparently from the bars next door.

The race was a bit of a disaster. Any lessons I had learned from Hong Kong the previous year, about the challenges of going from a Washington DC winter to tropical temperatures, had apparently been forgotten. I was fine for the first half of the race but as the sun came up it took a toll on me. I was feeling the effects by around the 32km mark, and by the time I reached the Benjamin Shears Bridge between 37 and 38 kilometers into the race, I was wondering if I was going to finish. That's not a feeling you ever want to have.

Approaching the Finish Line about an hour later than expected, the cheers from the crowd and the sight of a friend off to one side gave me the last bit of energy I needed to go across. Unlike my first race here three years earlier, I managed to stay upright this time, and moved on to collect my medal and finisher's t-shirt. Before I could figure out how to get to the meeting point where I was supposed to find my friend, though, a wave of dizziness told me I should sit down before I fell down.

After a few minutes of being seated I made my way to a First Aid tent, because something felt very wrong. The student nurses there seemed limited to just putting ice on people's knees and clearly did not know what to do with me. Finally, they put me in a wheelchair and pushed me to the real medical tent back near the Finish Line. As we made our way through the crowd I swore to myself that my second post-race trip in a wheelchair would be my last.

Now with real doctors and nurses, I was fixed up pretty quickly. They determined I was dehydrated and my blood pressure was low, which I probably could have told them, but it's good to get a professional opinion. They laid me out on a stretcher with cold packs on me, and put in two IVs to help rehydrate me. The nurses very kindly tried to call my friend, whose number was in the Emergency Contact section on the back of my bib, but he had drained his battery using the marathon's tracking app to follow me. It was not until he went into a Starbucks and plugged in that he saw the messages and missed calls, and came running.

I was fine, of course, compared to others in the tent. I saw a number of people getting loaded into ambulances, and there were a couple folks who seemed to have fallen and broken a limb. With about 50,000 people participating across the three events that morning, it was no surprise that there would be others worse off than I. After about an hour I was able to leave, not feeling great but at least able to walk, and it was time to start thinking again about what I needed to do to make the move to Singapore.

~

I returned for good on New Year's Eve, though I would go back to Washington DC for training in mid-January, giving me a chance to pick up the rest of my stuff and bring it over. As it turned out, my Uncle Jim, whom I hadn't seen in a couple years, passed through Singapore that month on his way to Australia. That was my first hint that I could expect visitors to my new home, something that happened almost monthly thereafter.

My apartment worked out very well. I had found it on the next to last day of my December visit, and had just enough time to transfer money from the US to pay the deposit before heading back home. It was in a great neighborhood with plenty of food and shopping options nearby, and the subway was about a 10-minute walk away, with only two stops to get to my office. Though it cost roughly twice what I had been paying back in the US, it was surprisingly cheap compared to a lot of other places where my friends lived.

In an unexpected turn of events, my friend Linh wound up moving to Southeast Asia a couple months before I did. The international development organization where he worked offered him an opportunity to work in their country office in his hometown of Hanoi, and so instead of being on the other side of the world, he was only a couple hours' flight away. That gave me an opportunity to finally visit Hanoi as a tourist instead of for work, and he had a place to stay when he needed a weekend away and wanted to come visit Singapore.

The job, and Singapore, started out really well. Even though the position had sat unfilled for months, the plan was to give me three months to get up to speed on our research studies and our clients. Other people would still cover the work where necessary, and the leadership team would run me through some simulated meetings and presentations before turning me loose on an unsuspecting clientele. Meanwhile, I had time to get used to my new city before I began traveling a lot.

As I got into the research material I was very impressed, and I wished I had had access to all this when I was teaching. In the meantime, I got to know the clients' backgrounds too, and I was pretty happy with the collection of companies with which I would be working. Most of my work would involve advising the Chief HR Officers at major Asian companies, and they were a diverse bunch. The industries ranged from banks, airlines, and telecom firms to government agencies and international development organizations. I could expect to have 40-50 clients at any one time, in seven countries stretching from Singapore up to mainland China, with new places to be added as we grew.

My probationary period went well, though I certainly had a lot to learn. Not only was this my first consulting job, it was my first real private sector job of any kind. Throw in the fact that I would be operating in multiple cultures that were all different from what I was used to, and I started feeling a little overwhelmed. I had to adapt my working style to meet this new environment, and that meant questioning some methods that I thought were best for me, something that is never easy. Fortunately, I had some good managers and colleagues who were patient but firm, and by the end of my probationary time I was ready to go.

The amount of travel required surprised me, though it should not have. I had always heard that business leaders in Asia prefer to talk in person rather than over the phone, and my clients did not care that I was in another country; if we were going to talk, they wanted to see me. While I could do some of the conversations by phone once I established a relationship with them, this job would be a lot different from that of my counterparts in our US offices, who did most of their out-of-town consulting by phone or videoconference.

It was a shock to my system at first. After a few months I was at the point where it was no surprise to travel somewhere different each week. I very quickly had enough visits to Hong Kong to enroll in their "frequent visitor" registration program, which allowed me to go through automated immigration gates rather than spending 45 minutes in line. By the end of May I had already become friends with one of the front desk managers at a Hong Kong hotel. In July I had my first "up and back" trip to Shanghai, which involved a 6-hour redeye flight up, two hours of a presentation and follow-on-meeting, then a 6-hour flight back.

The travel experience was different from anything I had done before. I soon achieved the highest status in the loyalty programs of my preferred hotel chain and airline, and I became in expert in managing points and miles, which would help my Grand Slam travel significantly. People often think that business travel can be glamorous, and in the movies I suppose it often is, but the reality was a little different. While I adjusted pretty well to my new schedule, the one area where it quickly took a toll was on my fitness.

~

Though my transition to Singapore and the private sector was generally going well, it took a long time before my running would become consistent. I had joined a gym immediately upon arriving and arranged to work with a trainer named Shehan who knew that my fitness goals would be focused on running. Working with Shehan helped bring a sense of accountability that I really needed, because I would need to workout before going to the office, and that meant getting up at 6am, which I am not famous for doing. When you know someone is waiting for you, though, you roll out of bed and go.

Shehan was patient with my changing schedule. Once I got beyond my probationary time and started traveling a lot, my workout schedule would vary from week to week. I was good about keeping up with the gym, but my actual running and marathon preparation was another matter.

I had made the decision not to run any marathons until the Cape Town race, since I knew I needed time to adjust to all the new things that were happening in my life. I think the lack of a race in the near future diminished my drive to get out and engage in serious distance running. The heat and humidity of the climate offered a further disincentive. The biggest problem I had, though, was not knowing where to run.

The last time I was in Singapore I was teaching at a university with open spaces, but now I was working downtown and living nearby, and had no good idea where to go for a long run. I had not found any running groups who could offer advice, but that was probably because I was not looking in the right places. A coworker recommended a nearby park, and that was good for a few miles, but running circles around it was not really what I had in mind. It took about 6 months before I found a running path I was really comfortable with, something that was mostly along the water, away from traffic, and that offered a variety of possible routes that I could use to adjust my distance.

Something still did not feel right, though. I was having trouble pushing myself to get out there. Maybe my brain was so taken up with all the changes, maybe my schedule was preventing any kind of consistency, maybe it was the weather, but for whatever reason, I just did not feel motivated. That worried me a bit, not only because I had an upcoming race in South Africa, but also because I still had three more Grand Slam races to complete after that, and I just was not feeling like running seriously.

As always, Ethan came through for me. I had talked with him about what was happening, and rather than just offering some advice, he sent along some motivation. A couple of American friends were visiting me for a few days late in the summer, and Ethan had them bring me a book called *Born to Run*. Written by Christopher McDougall, it tells the story of the Tarahumara tribe in Mexico, who appear to have unlocked the secrets of long-distance running. It was a great story about finding and meeting the tribe, and sharing their lessons with other runners to see what results they could come up. It was the perfect motivator, and I felt energized to get out there and get ready for Africa.

~

Choosing an Africa race for the Grand Slam took some time. I was trying to decide what kind of experience I wanted. Initially, I considered something in Kenya or Ethiopia, since so many of the elites come from there. After exploring some options there, however, I decided I wanted something with a little more infrastructure underneath it. I was reading stories from Nairobi about a lack of water on the course and limited emergency medical care, and I felt like I have enough to worry about with just running the distance. I did not want to add any other issues during the race.

For a short time, I considered a race in Egypt. Technically, it sits in Africa, though most people don't think of pyramids and the Sphinx when they think of Africa. I finally decided against it, though, in part because it was not quite the experience I wanted in Africa, and in part because unrest was breaking out in various parts of the country. I did not want to schedule a race only to have it be cancelled by violence, or worse, get caught up in it myself.

Friends who had visited Cape Town suggested checking it out, and a quick review showed that the Cape Town Marathon would take place at a good time of year. By September I would be finished with my probationary period at work, so taking a few days of vacation would be easier. Cape Town's location, at the southern tip of Africa, meant the race takes place at the start of spring, with cool temperatures. It easily seemed like the best option.

Traveling to South Africa was easier than I had expected. Singapore Airlines flew directly to Johannesburg, and depending on the day of the week either the plane continued on to Cape Town, or you transferred to a South African Airlines plane. I arrived in the morning, and thanks to my status with the hotel they had arranged the room early so I could go right in. As annoying as all the business travel might occasionally be, it would offer some useful benefits when I traveled for races.

As nice as people told me Cape Town would be, they also said it was a little dangerous, and the hotel staff seemed to confirm it. I was staying close to Victoria & Albert Waterfront, and the people on the front desk advised me of the safest path for walking there, though they recommended taking the hotel shuttle. I did some early exploring around the neighborhood, to find the Starting Line and local restaurants and such, and found that even though it might look a little rough at night, it still seemed okay.

I went to the race expo that afternoon and was surprised at how small it was. Held in the basement of a community building that was a little hard to find, it consisted of the race bib pickup and a single vendor. Race expos are usually a place where local stores and other distributors have a big presence, since so much of their target market will walk through the doors, but not here.

Over the next couple of days, I realized why. Cape Town holds a famous race, but it's not the one I was coming for. Since 1970 the Two Oceans Marathon has been run on the Saturday after Easter weekend. The main event is a 56-kilometer ultramarathon that runs across the Cape Peninsula, and the weekend's festivities are a big deal for Cape Town. Our race, in contrast, was not. Participation rates were lower, and it generally got much less attention. When I would mention to people that I had flown in for the marathon, they were generally confused because they thought the race is in March or April. "This is the other one," I would tell them.

My friends had not been wrong about Cape Town. There was certainly plenty to do there. While I would miss out on the safari that I might have enjoyed if I had gone somewhere else, I had landed right in the middle of one of the world's best wine regions. I spent Friday morning taking full advantage of that, with a tour of the Cape Winelands around Stellenbosch that included stops at three beautiful wineries and picking up a couple nice bottles to bring home. While I normally stop drinking alcohol by Wednesday before a race, I was very happy to make an exception this time.

Off the coast is Robben Island, famous for serving as the political prison where Nelson Mandela and so many others were held. The tour of the prison is very eye-opening, and though I certainly remember the apartheid era, I still learned a lot I had not known. Our guide was a former prisoner, and that in itself was pretty sobering.

The day before the race I did something that might not have been the smartest move: I went on a whale-watching trip. The trip itself was great, and though our skipper was careful to follow the rules and not approach too close to the whales, the whales did not feel constrained by the same rules and would approach our boat. Seeing these creatures up close – and knowing they could probably flip our boat if they felt like it – was a highlight of the trip. The only downside, though, is that I get seasick, and even though the sea was fairly smooth, my stomach wasn't. Getting sick like that is a good way to dehydrate, which is the last thing you want to do the day before a race. It's also a good reminder of why I joined the Air Force rather than the Navy or Coast Guard.

~

Finally, it was race day. I had planned things pretty well, choosing a hotel that was within walking distance of the Starting Line. I had checked it out in advance, just to make sure I knew how to get there, but as it turned out I could just follow the crowd.

We had an early start and it was still dark out, but there was a pretty great energy in the air. Everyone was very excited. Things seemed well organized, and we took off on time. The race would start off downtown, then move out into residential and commercial areas on the outskirts of town, then come back through downtown and head for the coast, where we would finish. I didn't know how scenic the route would be, but at least I would get to see some different parts of Cape Town.

Friends had told me for years that Cape Town was a pretty place, and I was looking forward to finding out. Running in the dark around the downtown, it looked more or less like any other city before dawn, but as we moved around I started seeing what my friends had been talking about. Since arriving I had been fairly limited in terms of where I went, but now I was going to see a lot more of the city.

The runners seemed to spread out pretty quickly, so after a few kilometers there was not a lot of bunching up. The roads in the early going had mostly been blocked off, so we had the entire street to spread out. Some of the streets would be a bit narrower in the later going, but by then we were far enough apart that it was not a problem.

About a quarter of the way through the race we were running through a residential section and I heard a group approaching from behind. I thought I was hearing people cheering along the road, but it was actually a group of runners singing in a language I did not recognize. There are eleven official languages in South Africa, and the only one I speak is English; this definitely was not that. There were about 20 runners, with one in front leading the singing, and if they were not all in step as they passed me, they were pretty close. I have no idea if they came from the same tribe out in the hinterlands or if they were a group of bankers from Johannesburg, but for me this was the moment I was hoping for in the race. This was my "running past the Eiffel Tower," my

"Christ the Redeemer watching over us as we run through Rio." This was Africa.

The temperature was very reasonable, with clouds overhead and even some occasional light rain, but nothing that should cause a problem. Even with the cool temperatures, of course, I still needed to rehydrate. As I stopped at a water station midway through, though, I got a bit of a shock.

Coca-Cola was one of the race sponsors, so it had not been a surprise to see Dasani water at the earlier stations. A drink company that sponsors a marathon will provide the drinks; that's not unusual. The surprise waiting for me at this station was that, in addition to Dasani water, there were small cups of Coca-Cola waiting for us, too.

At a well-organized race, you typically will see a mix of both water and isotonic sports drinks at stations. The water is for hydration, while the isotonic drinks – think Gatorade, Powerade, or 100-Plus, something like that – help replace the electrolytes lost through sweating. Runners will debate the merits of isotonic drinks, but I have never heard anyone discuss having carbonated soft drinks in a marathon. While the Medoc Marathon in France is famous for offering wine at their drink stations, the suggestion to "have a Coke and a smile" would have never occurred to me. I have to admit, though, that while there may not have been much nutritional benefit to it, it sure did taste good at that point.

One nice aspect of the race was that, despite its relatively small size, it was very international. Not only did we have plenty of runners from other African countries, we also seemed to have quite a few from Europe and Asia. Running through a residential area at one point, I passed a young Japanese man running in a kimono. I was happy that I was the one passing him, since being passed by someone wearing that much clothing would have been pretty demotivating at that point. We exchanged nods and I moved on. I saw him and his friends on the plane the next day and tried to chat with him, but he did not speak English. I hope at least one member of their group did, because if not they may have had a difficult time getting around Cape Town.

As we maneuvered around the outskirts of town, past hospitals and industrial areas, the crowd of runners became very spread out. We were in an open area, with the roads all blocked off, so everyone was running their own pace, and the size of the field of runners was small enough that we could keep each other in sight but not be running on top of each other. That would change as we got back into the city center.

The weather had been threatening us all morning, and as I got about two-thirds of the way through the course, it seemed to pick up steam. The wind was getting stronger, darker clouds were moving in, and it was becoming obvious that we would be getting wet before the race was over. I was not too concerned – I had run races in the rain before – but I always get nervous about slipping and getting hurt, and since this was one of my Grand Slam races I wanted to be especially careful not to knock myself out of the race before reaching the Finish Line.

Coming around the edge of town along the highway, we slid back into the city streets, and the nature of the run changed. On the plus side, we had spectators again, even if they were mostly just people on their way to church or heading to a market. Still, it is always good to have people along the sides of the road to offer some motivation. I started to see spectators whom I had seen earlier in the day; one guy in particular carried a large stuffed pig, which not only made him stand out but also made me think of Ethan.

The downside to the city streets is that we had to share them with traffic. Cape Town had blocked off the streets in the early miles, when it was dark out and most people were still asleep, but now that the city was up and moving around, we would not have exclusive use of the roads. The police had blocked off one part of one lane going down a major street, so we started to bunch up again as we not only had less space but also had to run more carefully while we watched the traffic. Some of the drivers had not gotten the word about what was happening, and while the local police seemed to be attentive, I did not want to put my fate entirely in their hands. Vigilance became the watchword as we made our way through a high-traffic area back toward the city center.

I had not spent much time in the downtown area, and what little bit I had seen had been mostly in the dark as we started. Coming back through in the daylight, I realized just how nice this part of town was. Emerging from the traffic and coming back onto some roads that had been closed for us, the run took on a different tone. The older buildings that had been kept up were much nicer that the simple, government-style buildings I had noticed earlier. The landscaping around them was nicely maintained, and there was a quaint style that made me think of this as "Old Cape Town." Running through these quiet streets, particularly in the historic area around Greenmarket Square, seemed like a very pleasant way to spend a Sunday morning.

Other runners seemed to agree, as the mood had changed. Whereas before, people had seemed a bit grumpy and focused along the streets we were sharing with cars, here there were a lot more smiles and nods to each other. While the weather was not really cooperating, and the arrival of more clouds and some sprinkling suggested we were about to get hit with some real rain, the neighborhood around us put people into a good mood.

I had chosen to wear my Republic of Singapore Air Force running singlet for this race, and that caught the eye of an older South African runner who was overtaking me. The back of the jersey simply said "Air Force," and as he passed me he asked, "Which air force?" "Singapore," I said between breaths, trying to keep my pace going as we started up a small hill. "Oh," he said, "what do you fly there? F-16s?" "Yeah," I replied, "C and D-models." "Nice," he responded, "how long have you been flying?" Since he had already decided I was both Singaporean and a fighter pilot, and since I was far into the race and pretty tired, I did not want to go through all the trouble of setting the record straight. "Well," I said, "I'm a retired lieutenant colonel, so quite a while." That seemed to be the answer he wanted, as he broke out into a big smile and replied, "Great! I used to fly here, but that was years and years ago. Keep your nose up!" With that, he took off, and I was happy to have made his day.

As we moved out of the historic downtown and closer to the ocean, I started feeling the effects of the run. I seemed to hit the wall at around 32 kilometers, which was pretty normal. We had a U-turn around this point, so I could see the runners on the back end as they ran along the water, while I was on the front end, running along a road. Loops like that can have a depressing effect on me because, when I cannot see the actual U-turn, I feel like I have a long, long way to go before I will be where those folks are. In reality, it may only be a couple of kilometers until the turn, and in the grand scheme of things that is not very far, but when I contrast what I know intellectually with what my eyes are telling me, it is usually my eyes that win.

We had moved off the road now and into a small park. The runners had spread out again coming through downtown, but now we seemed to bunch up some more as we ran along a fairly narrow path and a lot of people started slowing down. The crowd of runners I saw around me now were the people I would probably see until the end, with some minor shifts in position but probably nothing drastic, unless someone got close to their limit and started drifting back. The odds of anyone pulling far forward at this point were pretty slim.

As we made the U-turn we found ourselves on a path running along the edge of the ocean. This was not a nice sandy beach area for lying out in the sun, but instead was a very rocky space with heavy waves crashing up and spraying us. Mother Nature decided to have some fun with us, because this was the point where the clouds finally opened up and the rain hit us. While it was not a heavy thunderstorm, the steady downpour combined with the ocean water hitting us certainly helped keep our body temperature down for the rest of the run.

We had a few dedicated spectators, but by this time most of the people we saw were simply out for a stroll with their family. As we came around a curve along the boardwalk, it was obvious that some of the people walking around were very confused by the tired runners with numbers on their shirts. It was clearer than ever that this race was not the big one that Cape Town residents would be familiar with. Things would be different during the Two Oceans race in a few months.

Turning around that curve, I could see our destination in the distance. The Finish Line would be at the stadium built for the 2010 World Cup, so long before we could see the Finish Line banner, we could see where it would be. Seeing my target always helps, so I picked up some speed and did my best to move faster. It was obvious that I would not be running a personal best today, but I was determined to finish in less than five hours. The only times I had exceeded five hours had been during my two bad races in the high-heat conditions of Hong Kong and Singapore, and I refused to be that slow in this climate.

Turning toward the stadium, I put myself on what I thought was a direct course to the Finish Line. I had not counted on the twists and turns through the parking lots, so just as in my very first marathon four years earlier, I kept asking myself "where is the turn to the Finish?" Finally, as I came around a turn to the left, I saw the banner only about 150 meters in front of me. With a final push I finished strong, and crossed the line in 4:53:58.

Moving beyond the Finish Line, I was joined by a runner named Shaun who had come in right behind me. We high-fived, and I asked if he was from Cape Town. It turned out he was down from Johannesburg, and he was going around the country to do a race every weekend. He asked where I was from, and when I told him Singapore he got very excited. "Wow," he said, "you're the first person I ever met from Singapore." He insisted we get some photos together and he introduced me to some folks as his new friend from Singapore. I have a feeling if he ever actually visits Singapore he will be surprised to find that nearly all of the people there do not look like me.

Shaun was an interesting fellow. Along with his goal of racing every weekend, he was finishing every race by doing cartwheels across the Finish Line. In fact, as I looked at photos later of myself coming over the line, I could see him behind me preparing to do a cartwheel. This was all part of an effort he was making nationwide to motivate people facing serious problems, showing them they could pull themselves out of trouble. Shaun had gone through some challenges of his own in recent years, and turned to running as a way to get past them. His efforts led to him becoming very well known in South Africa's running scene, and over the years since then I have seen him on magazine covers and receiving awards. He is also now married to another runner, with an adorable baby daughter, and he has indeed taken his life in a great direction.

As we parted ways and I took a final turn around the finishing area, the sun started coming out and I realized I felt pretty great. In a few minutes I was going to have to figure out how to get back across town to my hotel, but for now I was content to just walk around and take it all in, cheering on other runners near the Finish Line and congratulating those who had crossed it. The race ended on a festive note, not because there were booths and vendors and food and tens of thousands of people, because those were not there. Instead, it was festive simply because of the happiness pouring out of people who had a pretty great day. For me, of course, there was still a sense of wonder as I walked around.

I was in Africa, and I had gotten here through running. I could not decide which of those statements was more surprising.

~ 8 ~
Australia

Blackmore's Sydney Marathon
Sydney, Australia
September 22, 2013

I had gone a long time between races when I made the move to Singapore, but now I fell back into my old pattern of running races a little too close together, and while that may not have been good for me, I had fun doing it.

Following my 2011 experience in the Standard Chartered Singapore Marathon, I was not too excited about running it again, but I also did not like the feeling that the race had beaten me. I decided that I would run the December 2012 race and then make that my last one, finishing on a high note rather than on my back in the medical tent. So, ten weeks after Cape Town, I was once again at the Starting Line on Singapore's Orchard Road.

My plan for this race was simple: finish upright, without a medic hovering over me. To that end, I was unworried about timing or any other goal other than finishing. I had a pretty good idea of how quickly I could run without seriously hurting myself, so I aimed for that. I ended up finishing slower than planned, but for a good reason.

Nearing the halfway point I passed a young runner, who then caught up with me a moment later. He started chatting, and asked me if I was running for a particular time. I told him I wasn't, and he asked if he could run with me. It seemed he had run last year but did not finish, and he was worried that if he ran by himself again, he would also not finish again. Whether he saw in me another amateur like himself who was just running for fun, or a middle-aged man who probably would not run very fast, I will never know, but I was happy for the company and we ran the rest of the way together.

It ended up being a very slow day, much slower than I had planned, even slower than the previous year by a few minutes. He was having some trouble and so we walked quite a bit in the last 10 kilometers as we came through Gardens by the Bay and across the Benjamin Shears Bridge. He admitted the bridge had brought him to tears the previous year and had been the point where he had to stop. I tried to get him to run a little more in the final two kilometers by pointing out the photographers, and looking at the pictures later you would think we were winning the race. As it was, I got him to kick it in during the final 200 meters, to the point that it seemed he would finish ahead of me, and I was not quite ready to give him that, so I picked up my own pace to finish together.

Incidentally, two years later I was watching for friends at the Finish Line of the same race, when I saw a familiar face for a split second. When I got home I looked up that young man's name in the results, and sure enough, there he was. Not only had he just run it again, he had finished about 90 minutes faster than we had in 2012. I still had his contact information from when I had sent him our photos, so I was able to write and congratulate him. We had not been in touch since 2012, and it was nice to know he was still running and was continuing to improve.

One of the reasons I ran the Singapore race was to be ready for a race coming up in January. Ethan would be visiting family in Vietnam and he wanted to run a marathon in Asia. We had chosen the Khon Kaen International Marathon in northeast Thailand at the end of January, so the marathon in Singapore fit pretty well into my training plan. We would meet up in Bangkok for a couple of days, then fly up to Khon Kaen for the weekend, and return to Bangkok for another day before I went home to Singapore and he went back to Vietnam.

Since I was the local person, and had traveled to Bangkok quite a few times already, I took care of the logistical arrangements. I settled the details of our hotels in both of the cities and the flights in between them.

Unfortunately, the one thing I never bothered to do was register for the race itself.

It was not until the night before leaving Singapore that I realized what I had done or, more accurately, had not done. The online registration had ended, so I wrote Ethan a "You are not going to believe this..." email. He replied that I should contact the race director, and not worry about it too much since they would most likely let me sign up onsite. He was right; with only about 700 people in the race, they could easily add one more person, and I registered at the race packet pickup.

The race itself was interesting. Khon Kaen is in the Issan region of Thailand, a relatively small city largely focused on agriculture. We started at 4:30am, passed through a Buddhist temple as the monks were starting their morning chants, went through a village at sunrise where everyone came out to sing and dance and cheer us on, and passed by some water buffalo on the highway. I committed the cardinal sin of trying something new on race day, as Ethan had brought coconut water and I drank that for the first time, but otherwise had a good day. I was still not as fast as I was in the US, and Ethan ended up beating me – as did a group of three women who appeared to be in their 60s who passed me near the end, chatting casually with each other – but I had a nice time.

As we progressed through 2013 I tried a half-marathon for the first time. Singapore has a springtime event called the Sundown Marathon, a race that starts at midnight. I had always thought it would be fun to run it, but this year I opted to try the half-marathon. It was a fun race that mostly avoided the long park runs that are so common in Singapore's full marathons, and the run was a great experience. I finished with a time of 2:14:07, which seemed decent for the conditions and which further convinced me that my body was not getting slower, I simply was fading under the impact of the climate in the later stages of the full marathons. If I could just keep that pace in the longer events I would be doing pretty well; the trick was to figure out how to do that.

I felt like my running was getting better. Part of it was finally feeling like I was settling into Singapore and into my job, and perhaps part of it was simply getting more used to the heat and humidity. The biggest improvement to my running, and my overall mindset, was about to come, though, when I finally quit running alone.

~

In late 2012 I met another runner and started running with him, but the truth was I felt like I was slowing him down. We went out together a few times before the Standard Chartered Marathon, and started that race together, but afterwards we never got into the habit again, though we did stay in touch. I mentioned to him that I was looking for new shoes and he suggested I talk to the manager at a particular New Balance shop. That led to a bigger change than just a new pair of shoes.

The manager, Kee Wee, got me into a great pair of shoes that offered some positive changes for me, but more importantly, he told me about the New Balance Runners group that met there every Thursday night. Running 5-10 kilometers each time, the group included marathoners as well as people running for the first time. I liked the idea of getting out there with others, because I always push myself more when I am with other people, so that summer I finally joined them on a Thursday night.

That first night, I ran with a group of eight people out of the larger group of roughly 35. We ran at a decent pace, one where we could maintain conversation, so I enjoyed chatting with them as we went through the streets and then along the river. We perhaps were not paying enough attention, as we turned around at the wrong bridge, earlier than we were supposed to. We were pretty surprised when we ended up being the first ones back, and we made up for it by continuing to run around the large lot by the shopping center.

Afterwards, a group of us went out to the food court at another shopping center next door. Coincidentally, it was the same place I used to go after my workouts at California Fitness during my time there in

2008-2009. There was a great sense of camaraderie in this group, and I knew I had made the right decision by joining them.

The following week, for whatever reason, I came in feeling like I had something to prove. There were only a couple people who were older than I, and I felt like I did not want to be labeled as an older guy, so I took off fast with the young group. There were four guys, who seemed to be fairly serious runners in their early-to-late 20s, and I was determined to run with them for the 10 kilometers we were running that night. I finished with them, but if you look at the photos from afterwards, it is obvious who had to do the most work to finish at that pace.

Over the coming weeks I got to know a few people pretty well, building friendships that have continued over the years. Despite having moved away from Singapore since then, I make an effort to schedule my business trips so I can be there on a Thursday night and join them for a run. As I travel for races in other countries, New Balance runners will often be there, so there is a chance to meet for a carbo-loading dinner the night before and hopefully catch each other in the Finish Area, or even see each other during the race. A lot of the faces have changed since I started, but the spirit remains the same.

One of the things that intrigued me about the group was that, while there were other foreigners there, they all came from Asian countries; I was the only westerner. Others might come in for a night or two, but I was the only one who stayed for the long-term. Somebody brought that up at dinner one night, commenting that people had been surprised when I stayed. I knew that plenty of westerners worked out in groups, but the gatherings I saw all seemed to consist of only westerners. I never understood that.

Running with a group helped push me to go faster at least once a week, and also provided some accountability that helped keep me honest about the mileage I was running each week. That helped a lot during the summer as I was preparing for the upcoming Sydney race. One of the big challenges I faced was the scheduling conflict with my work; it was not uncommon for me to be traveling somewhere else on a Thursday night. Later, I would start planning my trips outside of Singapore such that I would be back by Thursday evening, but for that summer, work was getting in the way. Unfortunately, the job was starting to seem less and less worth it.

~

Some changes at work, starting a year earlier, had been pretty disruptive. It all began when the Managing Director who hired me decided to leave the company and return to the United States just six months after I began. She had been really helpful in my transition to the private sector, and was a very supportive boss. As things turned out, she was not replaced for over a year, which put a lot of stress on the office.

Around the time she left, my job scope expanded, something I later learned had been planned all along but had not been shared with me. In addition to the one-on-one advisory work I had planned to do, I was tapped to lead small seminars for a group of clients in different cities a few times per year. In our US offices this was handled by a separate division, but we were so small in Singapore that we could not spare a position just for that role, and rather than flying people in from the US, the plan was for me to do it. We would later add some training workshops to our offerings, something that in the US would also be done by a separate group, but in Asia would be done by me. That led to some tension in the office as co-workers and clients who had been counting on me before now got less and less of my time.

Just after the Sundown Half-Marathon, my reporting structure changed. My manager was going on maternity leave, so to cover for her they would put me under someone who had been recently added to the office, an individual who had been with the company for a few years in the US but had no experience in my particular field. We had very different views on how to work with Asian clients, and also on the hiring and development of the workforce in our office. I also had some concern about his ethics, as I could see him implying to clients and to other employees that he had a PhD like I did, when the reality was he had never finished his degree. As time went on I felt a growing unease as I went to work each day.

~

As the end of September approached, though, I quit worrying about the office and started focusing on the race. In general I felt better prepared than I had been for recent races, and I went to Sydney feeling ready to go. It was the beginning of spring there, the weather was supposed to be good for the race, and everything I had heard told me I would have a great time.

One of the best parts of the Sydney race was that Ethan would once again be joining me. As he pursued his own 7 continents goal he would require a trip to Australia, so this seemed like a great opportunity for him to check that off the list. He invited his friend Louise, whom I had run with a few times in the US, to come along with her husband, and they would be staying with another friend of theirs nearby so Louise could run the marathon as well.

The logistics of getting to Sydney were easy enough for me, with a direct flight from Singapore. My company had an office in Sydney and I had been there for training, so I knew my way around the central business district and arranged for a convenient hotel for Ethan and myself. My business travel and hotel loyalty program status paid off once again; we used points to pay for the hotel and took advantage of a "5th night free" offer, as well as an upgrade to a suite, so Ethan and I stayed in 5-star comfort for nearly a week at no cost.

The weather was a little cooler and much cloudier than we were expecting. With me coming from Singapore, and the others flying in from a hot summer in Washington DC, the temperatures took a little getting used to. We certainly welcomed that for race day, but it was not very helpful when we were playing tourist.

At lunch on the first day we found ourselves near Sydney's Chinatown, and the group wanted to try a Malaysian restaurant we had walked past. For me, coming from Singapore and working with clients in Kuala Lumpur, Malaysian food was something I had on a regular basis, and my first instinct was to go for something western. I realized, though, that finding authentic Malaysian food in the US was hard for them to do, so we headed inside. Of course, as the only non-Asian in our group, it seemed ironic that I played the role of food expert. That night we went out for a local dinner of kangaroo steaks, which made me feel a little awkward the next day when we went to a nearby wildlife park.

Featherdale Wildlife Park was one of the highlights of our trip. Located about 45 minutes from downtown Sydney via train and bus, it offered the chance to interact with local wildlife. My goal was to hug a koala, but once we were there I learned the law did not allow for that. Koalas are protected, as they should be, and while we could pet them, only the trained staff were allowed to hold them. We also got to feed kangaroos, which had learned how to interact with humans and did not seem inclined to punch or kick us. There were plenty of other animals I had only seen on TV that I finally got introduced to, and the day ended with me cradling a baby wallaby that seemed to want to come home with me. Say what you will about keeping animals in captivity, I think once people have a chance to see and interact with animals, they may be more inclined to participate in or contribute to environmental causes.

Sydney is a great city, and over the years it has been a good place for me to go when I need a "western fix" but do not want to make the 24-hour journey it usually takes me to get back to the US. For some reason, it has always felt like San Francisco to me. Maybe it's the laid-back attitude of the people there, maybe it's because it's on the water, or maybe it's just because I have always had great food there, but whatever the reason, a visit to Sydney is something I always enjoy.

~

Finally, it was race day. It was a quick trip across the Sydney Harbour to the starting area on the other side of the Harbour Bridge. The sun was just coming up as we left, and the temperature was a lot cooler than we expected. When we were out a couple days earlier I had picked up a cheap coat at a Chinatown market, something I could drop at the Starting Line that would be picked up by volunteers and donated to a homeless shelter. Ethan, however, was not quite so well prepared, and he got very cold, very quickly. We made it a point to keep moving so he could avoid getting too chilled.

The starting area was a large park, and it was quickly filling up with runners and their supporters. We moved down next to the water, where a walkway gave us a great spot to stretch and an opportunity to jog a bit and get the blood moving. As the sun came up the temperature became a little more comfortable, and it seemed to stop rising just at the sweet spot, where we were fine while waiting but would not be overheated once we started running.

As the starting time approached we made our way to our corrals. I was feeling optimistic about this race, so I had put myself with the 4:00 - 4:15 pace team. Ethan was a little unsure how his leg would hold up – he was still being bothered by problems with his calf in the later miles – so he placed himself farther back in the pack. We didn't know it, but our positions would be reversed within the first half of the race.

Getting into my zone, I ran into Louise and the rest of the US and Sydney folks. We snapped a few photos, then I turned my attention to a last-minute mental review of what was coming. Though I had been to Sydney before, much of the race went through parts of the city I had never visited, and so other than the first few miles, I had been having trouble visualizing what the route would be like. Thinking about it for a couple minutes before the gun went off did not really add anything to my understanding.

As the race began, we moved out pretty quickly. Having been in races with tens of thousands of people, the faster start of a somewhat smaller race like this one always catches me off guard. As I crossed the Starting Line, I experienced a technical glitch for the first time. Unrealized by me, my GPS watch had lost its connection to the satellites, so I basically had a high-tech stopwatch on my wrist until I could regain the link. Rather than looking at the runners crowded around me I was instead looking at my watch, but I somehow avoided running over anyone or knocking anyone down.

This was also the first race where I would run with music, and that technology worked better than my watch. I was using my iPhone, which was strapped to my arm, and hit "Play" as soon as I crossed the Starting Line. While most of my running playlist was high-speed, typically 120-160 beats per minute to help me move along at a fast pace, the first song on the list was the Olympic theme. Odd as that may sound, I have associated the Olympics with the Sydney Harbour Bridge ever since the 2000 Summer Games were held there, and it seemed only natural to listen to that as our early steps in the race took us across that landmark.

Between the new watch and the iPhone, I was dealing with more technology than I was used to. Even though I had trained with music a few times in the preceding months, I still was not comfortable with it. It was one thing to be worrying about my music when it was just me on the path, but it was another matter entirely when I was surrounded by thousands of other runners who wanted to get moving.

One of my arguments against earphones on others over the years was that they can block runners' awareness of their surroundings. Too many times I found myself in the early stages of a race trying to get around runners who seemed to have no idea that anyone was around them, or worse, were spending more time focusing on their music player than on avoiding other runners. As I got started, trying to hit the right switches and fix my satellite problem, I realized I was doing exactly those things I did not like from others. I figured out pretty quickly that I needed to cut back on the technology in the future.

The first few miles went very nicely. We came across the bridge and into the downtown area near Circular Quay, and after a few twists we found ourselves moving away from the water and along the edge of the Botanical Gardens. Traffic was blocked so we had the streets to ourselves, as well as having a small crowd of spectators during the early hours.

Moving farther on brought us to Hyde Park, which happened to be across the street from our hotel. The footing was a little tricky through here, I felt, so I was watching my step carefully and making a note of it, as I would be a little more tired when I came through on the reverse run. I was a little concerned about crowding in this space, as we were running along the park paths rather than the wider streets. By this point, though, we had spread out enough so that we did not get too bunched up until we hit the midpoint of the park, thanks to an unusual feature.

As we had walked around town the previous few days we had noticed a temporary bridge over William Street, which runs through Hyde Park. I had just assumed that was for pedestrians to cross the street without disrupting the runners, but instead it was a path for the runners to get across the street, which still had cars on it. It used ramps rather than steps so it did not really disrupt your stride, but it did create a short bottleneck as the runners flowed over it. Once again I made a mental note for the return trip, though I figured by then we would really be spread out and it would be less of an issue.

Coming out of Hyde Park we made a left, and that took us into the Oxford Street area. The neighborhood is known for its nightlife, and some of that life was still making its way out of the clubs as we came by. There were a few spectators along the street, but quite a few of the people we saw were coming out of nightclubs and making their way home, a little after 8am. As they saw us running through the streets, and we saw them just finishing their night out, both groups seemed to be thinking, "what's wrong with those people?"

Oxford Street had a bit of an upward slope to it, which was the second uphill area we faced, the first being a slight rise coming away from the harbor. The marathon route was not hilly, merely having a couple areas with a small rise, along with a sharp hill that would come much later in the day. After Oxford Street things would stay flat until we came back, at which point we would be heading downhill, and by then I knew I would certainly be ready for that. I had walked along Oxford Street before so the slight rise did not surprise me. What did surprise me, though, was Ethan passing me.

Before flying over to Sydney, Ethan felt like he might run more slowly than I would so the plan was for us to start near different pace groups. What we found, at least in the first miles, is that he was going out faster than I was. Whether he would be able to keep that going until the end remained to be seen, but he went past me on Oxford Street and kept on going.

Turning away from Oxford Street, we left most of our spectators behind, both the intoxicated ones and the sober ones. Our path twisted around some of the venues that were used for the 2000 Olympics, including Allianz Park and the Sydney Cricket Grounds. Things were pretty quiet along here; not many spectators, came out to cheer us on, probably due to the limited public transit and the road closures.

Before long, we moved into the parks. We would spend a significant portion of the morning running through Centennial Park. It was an in-and-out path, which meant we saw people exiting as we were entering. I was feeling very jealous of them, wishing I was as far along as they were, but as Ethan reminded me years ago, I need to run my own race rather than worrying about what other runners were doing.

I am not a big fan of running through parks, unless there is some beautiful landscape to enjoy. We do this in Singapore, with an out-and-back run through East Coast Park, and it is simply the most boring part of the race. The same was true with Centennial Park. Sydney has a lot of interesting neighborhoods and it would have been nice to run through them instead. I understand that cities may hesitate to shut down too many roads to accommodate an event, but if New York City can do it, I do not understand why other cities feel they cannot. I have a lot of respect for race directors, who are doing their best to create a course that keeps everybody happy.

As we passed through the park we were on a bit of a loop, so I watched carefully for Ethan along the areas where those running out passed by those running in. I never saw him, so I had no way of knowing if he was already a couple miles ahead of me, or just a few hundred yards. Wherever he was, I just hoped his leg was doing fine.

Coming out of the park we largely retraced our steps back downtown. Rather than clubbers near Oxford Street we instead saw people heading out to brunch and families pushing strollers, pointing out "the crazy running people" to their kids. Temperatures were rising, though they were still nowhere near Singapore levels, and the humidity was low, so all in all the environment was still good. We moved into Hyde Park, went over the temporary bridge again, and without tripping along the sidewalks I managed to find myself on the streets leading back down toward the harbor.

The business district was a good place to run, since the tall buildings around us created enough shade to bring the temperature down. The roads sloped gradually downward as we moved toward the water, and though there were only a few people cheering us on along the streets, I could hear the crowd down below. Things were looking good.

As we got to the Circular Quay area, the marathon route seemed to pull a bait-and-switch on us. I could see runners in their final steps, circling the harbor and making their push for the Finish Line at the Opera House. There was a crowd cheering them on along the path, with the runners making their way through the gauntlet of supporters. It was something I looked forward to, but it was not my time yet, as I still had a left turn to make and a few more miles to cover before I could reach the point where they were.

With the Finish Line tantalizingly in sight, the race route took us back away from Sydney Harbour and around Darling Harbour. Rather than just running along flat roads, though, the city had closed off an elevated highway for us, and the fact that it was elevated meant we had a steep hill to climb. At this point in the race, the last thing my legs wanted was a hill.

Just as we were climbing the ramp onto the highway, the temperature was climbing as well. We were approaching noon, and while the heat was nowhere near Singapore's norms, it was a lot hotter than it had been at 7am. The lack of supporters and the discouragingly large number of walkers were slightly compensated for by the great views the elevation afforded us. I kept trudging along, running slowly but still keeping to my pledge of not walking, and quietly cursing the whole way.

We dropped down into a neighborhood for a brief turn, then were back up onto the highway and toward downtown once again. The fact that this time would be the last time we would aim for the harbor helped boost my speed a bit. I could not see the Finish Line from where I was, but I could feel it calling to me.

Coming back down from the highway I started moving through an older, quieter part of town without too many runners around me, and I had a chance to reflect on my running this day. I was starting to realize that living and running in Singapore was not leading to the benefits I had been expecting. My assumption had been that running in a harsher climate would be an advantage when I got to a nicer climate, allowing me to be a speed demon when I got somewhere with lower temperatures, much like athletes train at high altitude so their performance improves when they get back to lower altitudes.

That was not happening with me, though, and I thought about that during the last couple of miles as I considered how I had been feeling up on the highway. It was certainly true that I was running better in places like Sydney and Cape Town than I did in Singapore, there was never any doubt about that. I knew, though, that I had definitely slowed down in the years since leaving the United States.

It occurred to me that, while the harsh Singapore climate could be toughen me up, I was counteracting that by not training as hard there. In other words, I was not pushing myself as much as I pushed myself in the US, running slower on short and long runs, and not running as many miles. The "harsh climate helps" theory was only going to work if I pushed myself as hard there as I had been before, and that simply was not the case. I was not sure what to do about it, but I figured I should finish this race first, and then worry about it.

Coming out of this older district I hit the water of Sydney Harbour, on the far side of the bridge from the Opera House. With the Finish Line sitting right next to that huge icon I could easily see it as if it was right in front of me, even though intellectually I knew I still had to run around quite a bit of the harbor before I got there. Still, just seeing the end provided the boost I needed. My energy levels picked up and I felt myself smiling and running stronger, though if I am being honest, the presence of the photographers probably contributed to that, too. I always try to look good for the pictures.

The morning's clouds had faded away, the day was beautiful, the crowd was picking up, and I felt great. Soon enough I was past the cruise ship terminal and coming around Circular Quay, passing through the gauntlet of supporters I had been envious of a little while earlier. As I made my way through the crowd I turned left across a cobblestone path I had walked many times before, but now was running as a marathoner.

Bursting past the shops and out of the crowd, I saw the path to the end that Ethan and I had explored the day before. In the shadows of the Sydney Opera House, a large banner reading FINISH flew over the path ahead of me. My arms went up, my head went back, my stride lengthened, a yell flew past my lips, and I crossed the Finish Line.

I had finished Australia. Now there was only one continent left.

~ 9 ~
Antarctica

Antarctic Ice Marathon
Union Glacier, Antarctica
November 14, 2014

To finish up the continents, I was going to have to go from the equator to the bottom of the earth.

First, though, I was going to have to make some professional decisions. After returning from Sydney, my relationship with my manager at work had grown increasingly contentious. It was obvious we had very different agendas, and it did not seem like there was any way we were going to come together. We had finally hired a new Managing Director for the office, and he was great, but it was clear I would continue to be frustrated by my direct boss. As the consultants say, "People don't quit jobs; they quit managers," so I started looking around Singapore for other options.

A visit by our big boss from the US in late 2013 changed my thinking a bit. She told me I was on the company's "Top Talent" list, and people in other offices were starting to ask if I could transfer there. The reality, of course, is that I did not come to Singapore because of this company, but instead, had come to this company as a way to get to Singapore. I let her know that I appreciated hearing that I had a good reputation, but I planned to stay in Singapore, though I might not be staying with the company if something did not change soon. I had not planned to tell anyone about my issues with my manager, I was simply going to find another job and leave, but since she opened the door to that discussion I decided to walk through it.

Things moved pretty quickly after that. Within a couple days, she had moved me out from under that manager and set me up with someone in our London office who, though remote, was much more appropriate as a manager for someone in my specialty. I thought this sounded good, and I decided to try to bury the hatchet with my ex-manager, starting fresh and working together, since we still had to collaborate when it came to serving our clients.

Since this was my first experience in the private sector, though, I was unprepared for the retaliation that followed. Backstabbing, lying, gossip…all the hallmarks of insecure people that I had studied in my PhD, but now I was not simply studying them, I was on the receiving end. A bad situation seemed to get even worse. A couple of my best colleagues left in early 2014, and I realized it was time to start planning my own exit.

As with so many other professional changes, the decision came down to figuring out what was most important to me. I felt like I wanted to stay in Singapore, at least for now. I knew I wanted a job that required me to think and would be interesting, not just pushing papers around and answering emails. I enjoyed helping clients, and especially enjoyed leading small seminars for people who were really interested in the topic. Of course, having just had experience with a poor manager, I liked the idea of helping other employees have a better experience by improving the leadership skills of their managers.

That spring, in a few conversations with Linh over the phone or as he passed through Singapore, he finally asked, "Do you think it's time to start your own business?" This was something I always knew I would do, and in many ways my consulting experience to this point had been a rehearsal for what I ultimately wanted. Linh and I had talked a year earlier during a trip to Bangkok about the business model I might use in Asia, and now he was suggesting it might be time. Could he be right?

I started drafting a business plan, so I could at least know what it would take to get started and what my expectations should be. It became obvious that before I could flip the switch and open a leadership training business, there was plenty of work to be done. I needed to understand what topics would be most valuable in my markets, then develop them and have not only the training materials but also the marketing materials ready to go. I needed a website that looked professional and not "in progress." I wanted fresh content out on the web, such as through a blog and on Twitter.

Throughout the summer I started putting my plans together, not knowing when I would actually pull the trigger and go out on my own, but wanting to be ready. I had also applied for Permanent Residency in Singapore, not because I necessarily wanted to stay permanently, but because it would make it easier to create and run a business there.

The first change in plans came when Singapore rejected my PR application. They do not give explanations for rejections, but I figured it was either my age, or that perhaps they felt they had enough Americans. Whatever the reason, it meant I would need to find another way to establish my business.

The second change came from my friend Greg, who had been working at the US Embassy in Bangkok, and who asked me a great question: "If you expect to have clients all across Asia, do you really need to live in the most expensive city in Asia?" His point was well taken; I should look at other places to live. Bangkok would offer a lower cost of living, and I already knew some HR directors there who might be interested in my services. I considered Kuala Lumpur as well, but the city is a little hard to get around in without a car, plus I never felt as comfortable there despite having some great friends in the city. I decided that when the time came, I would make a move to Bangkok.

As things turned out, I ended up leaving the company about a week before going to Antarctica. With some changes in the company that had taken place in the summer and with more being planned for the following year, it seemed like this would be a good time to make a change of my own. I also was not sure that my company would support me being away for two weeks that late in the fourth quarter, with a chance I could be delayed even longer, so rather than fight that battle, I decided to move on so I could put those concerns behind me and focus on running.

~

Throughout the year between Sydney and Antarctica I kept up a regular running plan, and tried to figure out what I could do to prepare for the Antarctica race. The most important thing was keeping up the mileage. Anyone who can run a marathon should be able to run the polar races, so I just needed to make sure I could still run a marathon.

In late 2013 I decided there was not enough time between the Sydney Marathon and the Standard Chartered Marathon in Singapore for the latter race to be a good idea. Plus, I had pretty much decided that 2012 was my last time with that particular marathon. However, they also run a half-marathon that day, and my friend Azhan from Malaysia was interested in running, so we decided to sign up for it. To be honest, I hate just standing on the sidelines while my running friends are gearing up for a local event, so it felt good to get out and run it with him.

It was an unusual race in that part of it went through an underground parking garage. I had run through tunnels underneath a harbor in Hong Kong, but this was my first parking garage. My most vivid memory of that entire event is the beeping of all the GPS watches losing their connection to the satellites. The rest of the race was pretty standard, and it was fun to run with Azhan. We had been talking about it since he had started running a couple years earlier, and it was nice that we finally made it happen. My friend Zuoren was waiting for us near the Finish Line, and all in all it was a great day.

That half-marathon was a good addition to my training for a big race the following February. Fate had been kind to me, and out of the 300,000 or so people who applied for the lottery to get into the 2014 Tokyo Marathon, I was one of the lucky 36,000 to make it. The race is one of the Abbott World Marathon Majors, and I had started thinking that my post-Grand Slam goal would be to run all six Majors, so this would be my second one after New York.

The Tokyo Marathon is a wonderful race. Held in late February, the temperature was pretty cool; in fact, a snowstorm the week before the event had us worried it might be affected. Distance running is a big deal in Japan, plus this is one of the Majors, so the crowd of spectators was very energetic and stretched from the Start to the Finish. The race itself winds through the city, unlike so many races that go out onto highways or spend a lot of time in a park. I have always liked Tokyo, and this was a great way to see it.

Unlike my previous races in cooler climates, I felt like I performed well in the Tokyo Marathon. The temperature was just above freezing, so that probably helped, but I also felt well prepared for this. I ended up finishing in 4:32:37, which might not sound like an especially fast time, but it is the fastest I have ever run in Asia. Five years after my first Hong Kong race, I had finished a minute and a half faster, reinforcing the idea that my slowdown in recent years was not due to age.

Three months later I had a chance to run a race that had been on my list for years. Singapore's Sundown Marathon would start around midnight and offer the marathon experience without the sun beating down on you. After running the Half Marathon the previous year, I was ready for the full distance. The timing had never been right for me to do it before, but now I finally had the chance.

While running at night was certainly different, I am not sure how much better it was for me. The humidity at night is still high. Edmund Lim, who led the New Balance Runners, had also pointed out to us that without the sunlight it took longer for our sweat to evaporate, and since that's where the cooling effect comes from, we could expect our performance to be off and our times to be slower. I found myself getting sleepy around 2:30am, but kept pushing forward because Zuoren planned to be waiting at the Finish Line, and if he could be there at 4:30am, the least I could do was actually get there. When I arrived at the Finish Line more than five hours after starting, he was one of the few spectators standing there waiting. That, to me, is a sign of true friendship.

As spring turned into summer and summer turned to fall, I did my best to get physically and mentally ready for what was to come in November. One huge milestone on the way to the Grand Slam was to first complete a marathon on all 7 continents. All these other races around Asia were fun, but they were not getting me to my goal. It was time to head south.

~

Getting to Antarctica from Southeast Asia can be a marathon in itself. The runners would be meeting in the town of Punta Arenas at the southern tip of Chile, so my plan was to arrange a round trip between Singapore and Santiago, then set up separate flights between Santiago and Punta Arenas. I needed some flexibility in my tickets because there was always a chance of getting delayed if the weather in Antarctica turned bad. The 2013 marathon had been stranded at the Union Glacier race site for a number of days before they could get back to Chile.

I had started looking at flight options in January, and had even locked in some frequent flyer award flights to get me there. As it turned out, those flight schedules fluctuated over the months, so I had to go back and start over. Most of my flights would be on award tickets, which cut the cost dramatically, though some of my South American legs would be paid for. Still, I saved a few thousand dollars over the cost of buying all the tickets.

There was still a cost, of course, but it was in time rather than dollars. When you book award tickets you generally do not have as many options as you would if you were paying for them. Add in the fact that nobody seems to fly directly from Southeast Asia to South America, and I was going to be taking a pretty roundabout path to get there.

I flew from Singapore to Taipei, a 5-hour flight aboard Taiwan's Eva Airlines, then connected to Eva's overnight flight to New York. I had booked early enough that I was able to get a good deal on award seats in first class, so a flight attendant helped make my bed and provided pajamas for my nighttime flight, leaving me reasonably well-rested when I landed in the US. I had about a 6-hour layover at JFK International, where I managed to get kicked out of some airline lounges as they closed for the night, and then around midnight boarded a flight to Panama City.

Once I got to Panama I had another long layover, not quite enough time to get out and visit the city, but certainly enough time to visit the airport food courts. I discovered a Cinnabon, which is a wonderful food outlet that makes airports smell really good, but which had not yet moved into Southeast Asian markets. We had landed around 6am, so I had to stalk them for a while until they finally opened for the day.

One more flight got me to Santiago around 9pm, 36 hours after leaving Singapore. Naturally, my bag with all of my polar gear did not arrive with me. I had a set of running gear in my carry on, but the heavy parka, boots, gloves and other daily wear I would need in Antarctica were somewhere in Copa Airline's baggage system. I knew it had made it to New York because I had to retrieve it and recheck it there, so I hoped it had made it at least to Panama. The Copa employee at baggage claim took my report and told me there would be three more flights from Panama City before I took off for Punta Arenas the next morning, so I felt somewhat confident I would have my gear. I gave her my hotel address and asked that they deliver the bag to the concierge.

All I saw of Santiago that night was the lights along the city skyline and then my hotel room. After a long shower I was ready for a real bed. Had I been a little smarter, I probably would have arrived a day earlier, so I would have an extra day to relax before climbing onto another plane, and I also would have had more time to deal with things like missing luggage.

Waking up early the next day, I checked downstairs and found no luggage, but did find a message that my bag had arrived and was at the Copa office at the airport. That was not what I had asked for, but at least the bag was there. After waiting 20 minutes for a taxi, with my pulse and blood pressure rising the whole time, I started making my way through early morning traffic to the airport.

Once I got there I went toward the check-in counter, only to find that Copa's office was on the opposite end of the terminal. So I finally got some running in as I raced across the building and got waved out of a couple of restricted areas before finally finding the office. There was my bag, and now it was just a matter of running with it, and my other luggage, back across the airport to check in and make my way to the gate.

There were a lot of different kinds of people waiting for the flight. There appeared to be Chilean business folks heading south, Chilean families on a holiday trip, foreign tourists preparing to trek through Patagonia, and of course, a few runners. Aboard the plane I sat next to a couple from Poland who were heading to the marathon, and when we had a short stop at another city along the way, a number of other runners came together and started sharing stories of how they ended up coming to Antarctica. Arriving at Punta Arenas I shared a taxi with Lyn, a runner from Melbourne, and we were chastised by the driver because she was sharing a cab with a man while her husband was back in Australia. I am not sure he ever got over the scandalous nature of that fare, but I do know he talked himself out of a tip.

Our main hotel was mostly filled with runners and with NASA scientists who were making flights over Antarctica to gather data for a study. After getting settled I just hung out in the lobby where a lot of the runners were gathering. Two of the guys from California, Larry and Jerico, said some things that made me think we might know some of the same people, and when I looked them up later on Facebook, we indeed had three friends in common. It still amazes me that I can travel all the way to the bottom of the earth and meet people with whom I have mutual friends. The world really is a pretty small place.

I finally had a chance to meet Richard Donovan when he arrived to brief us on how the next few days would go. We had arrived on Saturday, and the plane to Antarctica was scheduled to go on Monday. We were watching the weather carefully, because the plane only leaves Punta Arenas if they know the weather will be okay for the entire round trip; they cannot wait out a storm in Antarctica. The flight time is 4½ hours each way, so waiting for the weather to be good during that entire window means delays are pretty common.

As it turned out, we were delayed by a day. That created some lodging problems, since most of us were in hotels that were already booked up on the day we were originally supposed to leave, and that meant we would be left out in the cold. Richard and his team had planned for this, however, and within three hours they had rooms for all of us around town. The next day, we left those rooms behind, and headed for the tents on Union Glacier.

~

The flight to Antarctica was aboard an old IL-76 Russian military cargo plane. It is owned by a charter company called Air Almaty, which is from Kazakhstan, and the crew consisted of pilots, navigators, and engineers from that part of the world with experience landing in frigid, snowy conditions. They fly into Union Glacier twice a week during the months the camp is open. We were in pretty good hands. It was a reasonably comfortable aircraft, with the front third consisting of old airline-style seats while the rest was cargo space. A nose-camera view of the landing was shown on a screen at the front, and that, combined with the feeling of rolling down a few miles of ice runway, slowing very carefully, was pretty intense.

We had our cold weather gear out of our bags because once the door opened we would be getting the full Antarctic experience. As we suited up and climbed down the ladder, I took my first steps onto Antarctica and was overwhelmed by where I was. Moving away from the aircraft I looked across an open plain in one direction, toward some distant mountains in another, and felt like I was in a National Geographic photo.

Very few people on the planet had ever been where I was, and I knew this was the beginning of an adventure I would remember forever.

The camp was only a few kilometers away and the vehicles they had for us needed to make two trips, so I chose to wait at the runway and watch the operations there until the second trip. The wind started picking up, and some high clouds seemed to be moving in, making me wonder what might happen to the weather, and to our races.

Our base camp was run by an American company called ANI, which operates the facility in the same location each year during the Antarctic spring, roughly from November through January. In addition to the tour packages they offer, such as trips to the South Pole and to a penguin colony on the coast, they are also the site for numerous expeditions, including skiers, mountain climbers, scientists, and of course, us. Their staff in Punta Arenas had briefed us and done a gear check for each of us there, and their team at Union Glacier would keep us safe and well cared for. They also groomed the course for the marathon and would support us with aid stations and medical care.

Once at the camp we got a safety briefing, and it was clear they were not kidding around. The first thing that caught my attention was the need to stay covered up outside. The cold could cause frostbite pretty quickly – we actually had a runner who unfortunately never got to start because of frostbite problems – and our eyes needed to be covered because the thin ozone layer above us allows lots of ultraviolet radiation to bounce off the snow and cause snow blindness, which is essentially a sunburn of the eyes. The other key thing was to stay within the black flags that marked the camp perimeter. The area inside had been checked to ensure there were no crevasses under the snow; the area outside had not. Since a crevasse could easily be a mile deep, I saw no need to go exploring beyond the black flags.

I was paired up in a tent with Samir, a doctor from New Jersey. Our tent was toward the back, about as far as you could get from the dining tent, and also about as far as you could get from the toilet trailer. The pup tent was double-layered and largely warmed by the 24 hours a day of sunlight that we had at this time of year. We were each provided with a polar sleeping bag atop a cot, and there was plenty of room for our equipment.

The tent itself offered some learning experiences. For example, I learned that if I wanted to make sure something did not freeze, I should put it with me in the sleeping bag. I had a pack of wet wipes that froze into a solid block, and Samir's contact lenses froze in their solution within their storage case. I also discovered why they suggested we bring a water bottle that we did not mind throwing away: getting suited up to walk across camp to the toilet trailer could be a real hassle, so they taught us how to properly use the bottle to pee in our sleeping bags. I have no idea if that knowledge will ever be needed again, but if it is, then I am well-prepared.

Not long after arriving, Larry, Jerico and I decided to go for a short run along the road back toward the runway. We knew this was a safe area, and there was even a convenient turnaround point marked by an artificial tree – "the only tree in Antarctica" – that the camp staff had placed a couple kilometers away. The run was a good chance to try out my shoes in the snow, and also get a feeling for running with the face mask and goggles, none of which I had much experience with in Singapore.

The clouds I had seen from the runway came in quickly while we were running, and high winds soon followed. The idea had been for us to land on Tuesday, run the marathon Wednesday, follow that with the 100K race on Thursday, then fly out on Friday. Mother Nature had other plans.

In the camp the winds were strong, but out on the race course they were even worse. We got the word there would be no running on Wednesday because conditions simply were not safe. We mostly spent the time in the dining tent, getting to know each other a lot better, and having discussions led by the camp staff and scientists about life in

Antarctica. It was a good way to spend the time. The meals were also really good; there was fresh food coming in every few days on the plane, and an entire continent that could serve as a freezer, so the excellent chefs there enjoyed a good stockpile.

I realized during those first days how lucky we were to have a group of such great people, because being in close quarters for an extended period could have been very uncomfortable with a group that did not mesh well. As I got to know everyone I was also impressed with how accomplished this group was. When I had been in Singapore I could say, with a certain amount of pride, "I'm going to run a marathon in Antarctica." Of course, once we were here, everyone was going to do that, and many had done so much more.

The group around me included ultramarathoners, Ironman triathletes, and semi-pro rugby players. There were people who had started their own companies, people who led nonprofit groups, and plenty of folks who had raised thousands of dollars for charity as part of this marathon. We had a crew from a Chinese television network documenting the 100K race of one of their athletes. As my friend Heather pointed out, "No one would be here if they weren't ambitious and accomplished." It was an amazing experience to be surrounded by such interesting people.

The weather lifted somewhat on Wednesday, and the decision was made that the 100K course was safe. This race would be run along a 10-kilometer course with 10 laps, and since it was closer to camp and not experiencing all the winds, Richard and the staff decided to run it first. Seven people were racing; there originally had been a few others who were planning to do both races, but they decided to hold off and just run the marathon. The winning time was around 13 hours, with the last two runners coming in around the 24-hour mark after conditions had seriously deteriorated, creating a new definition of perseverance in my mind.

~

Finally, it was race day. Friday arrived, and it was our turn to get out there. I had been getting a bit nervous in the days leading up to the race, but I was not the only one. Most of us had not run in conditions like this before, and many of us had training plans that looked great on paper but that had been disrupted by real life in the weeks before we arrived.

Though we had worn heavy parkas, snow pants, and boots around the camp, running was a different matter. When it came to shoes, most of us simply wore standard trail running shoes, typically half a size or a size bigger than usual because we were each wearing two or three pairs of wool socks. Some people had spikes they could attach to their shoes, but most of us did not. We wore three layers covering our bodies: a wicking layer to draw sweat away from the skin; a fleece jacket; and, on the outside, a wind shell consisting of a jacket and pants. All of our skin needed to be covered, so I also had thick outer gloves and a thinner pair of gloves inside those, a face mask known as a balaclava that covered everything except the eyes, ski goggles, and a knit cap.

The practice run with Larry and Jerico helped boost my confidence, but conditions were different for the race itself. We had clear skies and reduced wind, which were a blessing, but they made things warmer. That sounds great in theory, but one of the biggest challenges of the race is maintaining your core body temperature, getting neither too cold nor too hot. Get too hot, and you sweat so much that the two inner layers of clothes get really wet. Then let some chilly air in, and you learn an entirely new definition of "cold." That's what leads to hypothermia, and it can keep you from finishing the race and, of course, potentially kill you, too. With the temperature hovering around -25C/-13F, I wanted to be careful.

Once the horn sounded and we started, I was fine with my layers, but despite having practiced with gloves on, I had a lot of trouble opening the vents under the arms of my wind shell. When I started heating up, it was hard to release that from where it was trapped inside the layers. Fortunately I was able to get the front zipper open, and I cooled down. I had overdressed a little bit, wearing a cap on top of the full-face balaclava. I took that off occasionally and could feel the heat leaving through my head, but it was nice to have it available when the wind kicked in.

The balaclava was, as expected, the biggest clothing challenge. Covering the mouth as it does, it can make breathing difficult. I had practiced, but it is one thing to breathe through a mask on a treadmill in your Singapore condo, and it is another thing to do it during an actual race in Antarctica. I could feel the mask getting wet as I breathed out and I was concerned about ice forming, but for the most part I was okay, and I got used to the breathing after a while.

I had been concerned about my goggles fogging up, but the only time that happened was as I approached the final checkpoint with about 3 miles to go in the race. They not only fogged, they froze, and the support staff at the checkpoint was not sure how to clear them because they figured even warm water would just freeze again. That's when we discovered that hand sanitizer will melt ice and won't freeze up, and so I finished the race with the cleanest goggles out of everyone. Unfortunately, there was no prize for that.

Mentally, everything went very well. I never had the "why am I doing this to myself?" feeling that sometimes pops up during a race. I was excited the whole time, and during the back stretch of my second lap I caught myself yelling "I AM RUNNING A MARATHON IN ANTARCTICA!!!!!!" There was no one within a couple miles of me so at least I did not bother anyone.

The setting was beautiful. Sometimes it felt like you were running forward into a painting. After about 7 or 8 miles we were pretty spread out, and for large parts of the race I saw no one in front of or behind me. It was also absolutely quiet. I could hear my breathing, I could hear the crunch of the snow under my feet, but that was it. Combine that with not seeing anyone and it was like being this last person on Earth.

I have usually found I run faster in a race than in training, in part because I am surrounded by other runners and that helps set a pace for me. But here, there were only 47 of us, and since we were so spread out I had no one pushing or pulling me along. It was also a little difficult to keep my bearings. Distances are very hard to judge there – an ice field that looked like something we could walk to in half an hour was actually 20 kilometers away – so I tried to keep things realistic when I would see an aid station ahead. It was actually going to take me a long time to reach it, so I tried not to focus too much on such distant objectives.

The race consisted of two laps around a 13.1-mile course that had been groomed using a SnoCat before we arrived, and was marked with small blue flags to keep us on track. One thing we needed to watch for were those blue flags that were placed every few meters. These marked the course, and in addition to staying on the path so as not to add extra mileage to our run, we also wanted to avoid disappearing. Much as the black flags marked the camp perimeter, the little blue flags reminded us that the race route had been checked for crevasses, but everything outside the flags had not.

Running on snow is unbelievably hard. Though the course had been somewhat groomed, there was nothing smooth about it. SnoCat tracks, snowmobile tracks, other runners' tracks, melting and re-freezing, and being on a glacier that has been moving 3 millimeters per hour, all combined to make a very uneven surface. We were lucky it was sunny, because it meant you could see the biggest changes in the surface, but in that kind of light in a big white space, while wearing polarized goggles, there is not a lot of contrast and it is hard to judge the surface.

I also found that, once you step on the snow, you tend to sink in even as you're trying to push off, so it requires a lot more effort to just get your legs moving. Your toes sink in with each step, putting pressure on them and increasing the chance of injury. After about 14 miles I started landing on my heels instead, which is very different from how I had been running since changing my stride a year and a half earlier, but it was what I needed to do. During the second lap, when I was more familiar with the course, I found stretches where I really picked up speed, but I will admit that was not my normal condition.

Our support crew was very helpful. In addition to medical teams cruising by on snowmobiles looking for a thumbs-up, we had two manned aid stations and one unmanned. At the manned stations we had not only warm drinks and food, but also a half-igloo with a field-condition restroom. The need for that is based on the Antarctica treaties: anything created by humans – anything – needs to be boxed up and shipped out. That means you cannot just stop by the side of the trail when nature calls. Unlike my past races where people ducked into the bushes immediately after the start, there would be none of that here. Of course, there were also no bushes.

I did have a couple of physical issues during the race. During the last 3 miles of the first lap I developed some severe pain around the middle of my back, and I used my midpoint pit stop to stretch it out, and also take some ibuprofen. I also needed to change all my inner layers as well as socks, gloves, and headgear, because I was concerned they were too wet. As it turned out, when I stashed a second set of gear in the dining tent for that midpoint break, I forgot to include underwear, so I ran the final lap of the Antarctic Ice Marathon while going commando.

Lastly, starting around Mile 18, I had some early signs of dehydration. This was not good, since once you see the signs it means you are already dehydrated. Though the temperature was obviously very cold, we were sweating and losing moisture every time we breathed out, and staying hydrated is critical. I tried drinking more at the stations, and I checked in with one of our doctors after finishing, but it was not until 36 hours after the race that everything felt normal again.

This ended up being the slowest marathon I had ever run, but I really did not care. In the first place, my goal was to do this, not do it quickly.

More importantly, though, was a thought from my friend Nancy during our midpoint pit stop: "I have been trying to get here for years, why would I want it to end quickly?" To be honest, though, I was really looking forward to taking my only shower of the week after the race: one minute long, using melted snow, and it was the best shower I ever had.

The final mile was a wonderful experience, and I kept looking around as I approached the Finish Line, trying to take it all in. My back had been hurting as I ran over the rough patches near the end, but that all faded away. As I passed the 26-mile marker, the final two-tenths of a mile were among the greatest moments of my life. I was yelling as I ran, arms up as I crossed the Finish Line, and I could not believe that after pursuing this for years I had finally done it.

I had run a marathon on all 7 continents.

~ 10 ~
The North Pole
North Pole Marathon
Approximately 90 Degrees North
April 16, 2016

My original goal, set years earlier on my 44th birthday, was to finish the Grand Slam by the time I turned 50, but that's not exactly what happened.

As the Antarctic Ice Marathon was approaching in 2014 I was still on track to do that, but when I started making plans to leave my job and start my own business, I had to rethink that objective. The North Pole Marathon was going to cost about as much as Antarctica did, and with all the uncertainty about what 2015 would bring, I thought it was a bad idea to start writing big checks like that. As hard as it was to do, I decided to delay that race until 2016.

That was probably a smart idea. As planned, I had left my job just before going to Antarctica, and upon returning it was time to start building my business. While flying back I thought to myself, "I just ran a marathon in Antarctica; running a business will be no problem." The adventure had certainly been a confidence booster. As is my nature, I tried to hit the ground running once I got back, and as is the nature of business, there were soon some big roadblocks in my way.

My business plan was very optimistic. I had plenty of HR directors at major companies with whom I had been working, and I was sure they would continue working with me now that I was on my own. I also felt that, given the demand for training that seemed apparent in Singapore, people would be lining up to attend the workshops I was organizing. I was wrong on both counts.

It took a while before anyone would tell me directly, as people often have trouble being direct in Asia, but even though my clients had enjoyed working with me, they also enjoyed all the resources my old company had to offer, resources I did not have anymore. Now that I was moving into a new role, and doing so without a big company behind me, I would need to prove myself all over again before they would be willing to pay for my services. That was going to take some investment on my part, and so it was good I had not committed my funds early to the race.

The move to Bangkok proved to be one of the smartest things I did. My monthly living expenses dropped to about 20% of what they had been in Singapore, so the six months' salary I had set aside to get started could last a lot longer, and it would be a lot easier to afford the North Pole when I finally did go.

Despite a slow start, my business did start to pick up in the second half of 2015. In August I was hired to lead a workshop in Melbourne, Australia, which gave me the chance to meet up with Lyn, my fellow passenger in the "scandalous" Punta Arenas taxi ride. It was great to see her and spend a couple hours chatting, and it helped me realize what an interesting group of people I had joined, these Antarctic runners whom I would likely be seeing again around the world.

Even though I was not going to finish my Grand Slam goal in 2015, I still needed to keep running. One downside to Bangkok is that it is not as runner-friendly as Singapore had turned out to be. Before, I could run a couple kilometers along safe streets before getting to a path along the Singapore River, and from there I could easily run long-distance along a nice route. In Bangkok, the best running area I could find was a park near my home with a 2.5-klometer loop that gets really boring after a few laps, and getting there required running two kilometers along a very busy street with motorbikes driving on the sidewalks. I ended up doing more treadmill running than I should.

Still, I had a decent running year, especially in July at the Gold Coast Airport Marathon in Australia. Plenty of friends had run this – Singapore typically has the third-largest foreign contingent, behind New Zealand and Japan – and so I was happy to finally try it. The route was flat, the temperatures were cool, the crowd was great, and I surprised myself by running my third-fastest time ever, at 4:14:04. This was the fastest I had run since the 2011 Paris Marathon, and the fact that I could still get back to speeds like that told me that I still have some potential in me.

Nearly three months later I took on my third World Marathon Major, the BMW Berlin Marathon. I told people that my training had not been great in the intervening weeks, and that I was running this just for fun, not for time. I even told myself that. But in my heart of hearts I thought the course, weather, and spectators at Berlin might allow me to beat my Gold Coast time, potentially setting a new personal best and maybe even beating the 4-hour mark that was still a major goal in front of me. That was not to be. I started out strong – possibly too strong, actually – and slightly more than a third of the way through the race I felt myself falling apart. I recovered later on and finished, but it was a good lesson in managing expectations, and I learned that I should balance goals with reality a little better.

Obviously, a nice part of that trip was the chance to visit Berlin, which I had never seen before, and also the opportunity to take a few days in Vienna on the way home, which was another new city for me. One very nice surprise was that Richard Donovan also happened to be in Berlin for the race, supporting a friend who was aiming for the Irish Olympic team. I got to spend the evening after the race at an Irish pub with Richard and a bunch of very fun people.

Around the same time, I decided I should do one more race in the year. Even though I had sworn off Standard Chartered Marathon Singapore after the 2012 race, I realized it could be a useful part of my training for the North Pole. After all, I needed to get some long-distance runs under my belt, and I might as well get a t-shirt and medal out of the deal. The race was 9 weeks after Berlin, and while my recovery-and-train cycle would not be ideal, I figured it would be useful. In the end, I suppose it was good to get the distance done, and I managed to avoid landing in the medical tent this time, but the heat was brutal and took a lot out of me. It was one of my slowest times ever, and I limped away thinking that maybe three marathons in five months might not be a good idea for me anymore, at least not without a more rigorous training program.

As optimistic as I had been about my business, I was equally optimistic about my fitness training, and I was just about as wrong. In my mind, since I would be working for myself and setting my own schedule, I would be able to include fitness in my routine just like any other aspect of my work. That first year, though, involved so much business development work and travel that I often felt it was difficult to get anything else done. Even though my gym, Virgin Active, was across the street from my apartment, I found it challenging to set a regular fitness schedule.

One thing that helped was taking some classes. I had chosen Virgin Active in part because they had a room that simulated higher altitudes, and they offered circuit-training classes there. I started going once or twice a week, which helped a lot because it put something fixed onto my calendar and made me accountable. Of course, the training itself helped too; though my upcoming races were all around sea level, the altitude training helped build lung capacity that would be useful at any elevation.

Something unexpected happened early in 2016. Virgin Active put out a call for members to tell why they work out, and I had sent them my Grand Slam story. They called me up and said that they had selected my story, that they wondered if I could come in the following week for a photo shoot with their team from London, and that they would be offering me a free year's membership in exchange for being in their marketing.

This followed another opportunity that had come up from a travel company in Singapore called Flight Centre Active Travel. Since they were focused on traveling for such things as marathons, cycling events, and triathlons, they asked if they could do some interviews with me for their blog. In exchange, I would get some credit toward travel that I booked through them that could help me get to my future races.

I now had two companies offering travel and fitness support in exchange for sharing my stories in their marketing. This pretty much fits the definition of a sponsored athlete, something that was on my "bucket list." This is something that, as a child – or even as an adult – I never would have thought possible, and yet it was happening.

It was around this time that I was also selected to be an Ambassador for the Abbott World Marathon Majors. This was a new marketing program for them, and though it was starting out primarily as a social media campaign, it meant I would be representing the six biggest marathons in the world. Again, this was something I could not have imagined even a few years ago, and it helped me realize just how far I had come.

Of course, I still had some distance to go: the distance to the North Pole itself. By the end of March I made a point to wrap up all my work for my clients, and scheduled no events for a month after the scheduled date of the race. On April 3rd I climbed aboard an overnight flight to Oslo, Norway, where I would spend a couple days adjusting to the weather and time zone before heading farther north. After touring around for two days I went back to the airport, where I met some familiar faces from Antarctica, and some new ones as well, as we boarded the flight to the town of Longyearbyen on the island of Svalbard, midway between continental Norway and the North Pole. It was time to make this happen.

~

Without too much surprise, we found ourselves delayed. Just before arriving at Longyearbyen I had read online that the runway at Camp Barneo, our base camp near the North Pole, had cracked. The team from the Russian Geographical Society that managed the site needed to build a second one before we could fly there, and they were trying at a spot close to the original, so they would not have to move the camp. I could tell there was a good chance we would be delayed by a day, and considering we had a day's delay going in and out of Antarctica in 2014, I was ready for that.

Unfortunately, the day after we arrived, we got word that the new runway had also cracked while they were building it, and they would probably need to find a new location to start over. The Russians would need to identify a new spot from the air, and then everything would have to move. As much as we tried to ignore rumors, including those that came from Camp Barneo's Facebook page, we were disappointed by the news. People started thinking about alternate travel arrangements after the race, and some people who had planned local excursions around Svalbard after their return starting inquiring into options before we headed to the Pole instead.

Our briefing on Thursday the 7th confirmed our worries, but also gave us some hope. The new runway had indeed cracked, but it sounded like they could get a new one built fairly quickly once they identified the new location. Richard suggested we would likely go in on Monday the 11th with a return to Longyearbyen on the 13th, though there was a chance we could go in on the evening of the 10th. Based on when we would go and the conditions we would find, we might also cut our time there down to 36 hours; Richard had said we could be in and out in that amount of time if needed.

The briefing about the race itself was somewhat sobering. It was becoming increasingly clear that this would be a lot different from Antarctica. The terrain would be rougher with temperatures most likely a lot colder; in fact, it was -40 while we were getting our briefing, and this was where I learned that -40 is where the Celsius and Fahrenheit scales merge, so it is the same no matter how you measure temperature. Richard's plan was to mark a course about 5 kilometers long so we would do 8 loops, and depending on where we set up we might do part of that distance on one of the abandoned runways, which would be an easier stretch.

Following Richard's briefing we got a presentation from our physician about cold weather injuries. It included photos of problems past runners had experienced, and it was almost enough to make you not want to go. I wish I could have attributed all the injuries to dumb things people had done that I would never do – and there were a couple of those – but mostly they were just bad luck. It made me nervous, as there have been people who have been unable to finish due to their injuries, and I could not imagine having to come back here again. The travel is fun, but the expense is not something I could handle for the foreseeable future.

Our next update would be Saturday night at 7pm, and hopefully we would have good news. Logistically, I was not facing any problems yet. Unlike Punta Arenas, which had a lot of small hotels, rooms were much more limited in Longyearbyen. Richard had recommended we book rooms even for the nights we expected to be at the Pole, just in case we were delayed like this. If I did not need them, the money would just be wasted, but if we got delayed, it would be money well spent.

As far as my post-race travel went, if we got back on the 13th there was a chance I would still make my early afternoon flight back to Oslo. Richard would have someone bring the bags we left behind to the airport, so those of us who needed to get off the polar plane and onto a commercial flight could do so without having to go back to our hotels.

I was trying not to worry too much about my travel, since there was nothing I could do about it. I wrote the travel agent who set up my Norway flights so he could add a note to my reservation asking the airline not to cancel my itinerary if I did not show up, but instead just be ready to change me to another flight once I got back from the Pole. Once again, the value of flexible tickets was very obvious. I connected him with Ethan, who had volunteered to be my point of contact that I would call if I had a further delay and needed to make changes from the Pole. So far there was no impact on my return to Thailand, but I made sure Ethan had the information he would need to change that flight too, if necessary. Finally, I contacted my Oslo hotel and asked them to hold the room for my return trip even if I did not show up on the scheduled day. Everything was as set as I could make it.

It was around this time that I had a very interesting random encounter. In January I had read an article about Colin O'Brady, who was trying to set a record for the Explorers Grand Slam, which consists of trekking to the South Pole and North Pole, and climbing the tallest peaks on all 7 continents. I had wondered if I might bump into him at the Pole, and at breakfast one morning I heard someone talking about trekking and climbing, and realized it was him. Like us, he had already been delayed a few days, and it was causing some problems. The rest of his team was waiting for him at Mount Everest, and he needed to get there and start acclimating along with them so he could make that ascent. He ended up on the first flight that went into Camp Barneo, and a couple months later I saw he had finished his entire journey and set a world record.

With a couple days to hang out, I wanted to do some expeditions on the island of Svalbard. My plan had been to do something after returning but since I was unlikely to spend much time on the island after the race, I figured I should get it in now. Unfortunately, everyone else had the same idea. I wanted to take a dogsled tour, and the first one I could book was not until Sunday morning, the 10th. Of course, there was a chance that would be our departure day, but I figured we were more likely to go on the 11th, so I booked the 4-hour trip and figured if I was not able to go, then the wasted tour fee would just be part of my expenses.

I took the opportunity to stock up on a few extra equipment items, write some postcards, and sample some more of the Norwegian pastries I was becoming too fond of. It was nice to just stop and relax with no responsibilities; it had been a long time since I had done that. I had already done one short run along Longyearbyen's roads and figured I would do at least one more, and try out the hand sanitizer approach to avoiding fogging on my goggles.

Sunday morning I finally got out on a very fun expedition. I had decided to do a half-day dogsled trip rather than a full day because we would have another briefing at 7pm. This seemed like a pretty easy trip, since the dogs would be doing most of the work. We would hook up the dogs and then head out a few kilometers, just checking out the countryside. It seemed like a nice way to spend the morning.

The weather was good, with just a little snow falling and a bit of wind. Another tourist and I took turns driving the sled, which happened to be the lead sled with one of the guides aboard. I did better than I expected, but the only thing I really had to do was slow them down occasionally and try not to fall off. We saw quite a few reindeer and learned about the local geography. I was amazed to learn that the valley where we were driving actually melted in the summer and turned into a small river. I did not realize it got that warm.

Our dogs were well behaved and were very excited to get out and run. Our guide obviously knew what he was doing and used all the right commands to steer the dogs, while I was responsible for our speed. Among all the other unlikely aspects of this trip, I was now driving a dogsled somewhere north of the Arctic Circle. This was not something I had ever imagined myself doing.

Sunday afternoon, we got some news we absolutely did not want to hear: a new crack had appeared in the second runway, and it was bad enough they would need to find a new location, airdrop some new equipment, and start over. The earliest anyone could be going in would be the 17th, which was a week away. Richard said people who wanted to stay would still be taken in, those who needed to go home could come back next year at no additional fee, and more details would be provided at the evening briefing.

I had not even seen this myself yet; Ethan had texted me the information after he saw it on the marathon's Facebook page. I was about to walk from my hotel back down to the center of town, so those two kilometers gave me a chance to think it through. It was pretty clear that I needed to stay in Norway and try to go in. At this point, I was working for myself and had no events planned until a seminar in mid-May. Next year, anything could be happening; I could be involved in a contract that could not be put on hold, I could be back to work at a company that would not give me the time off, or something else could be happening that would not allow me to return.

I had already paid for the hotel in Longyearbyen and had a ticket to Oslo on Wednesday, so I would just stick with that. Rather than returning to Bangkok the following Saturday, I would instead delay that flight and find a way back to Longyearbyen and, perhaps more difficult, a hotel room. The extra flight and extra hotel nights were expenses I had not planned on, but in the long run it was cheaper than flying back here again next year. The answer was obvious: this was my best shot at this goal, and I needed to stay and take advantage of it.

Not everyone had that option. Parents needed to get back to their families, folks needed to get back to work, and so there was no way everybody could stay. Richard would go through all the options at the briefing that night, but for me I knew the only thing I needed to worry about was finding a laundry once I got to Oslo, since I would soon run out of non-polar clothes.

After the briefing I immediately went to work lining up a new itinerary. I set up new hotel rooms in Longyearbyen that were big enough that I could have other people stay with me and help me cut my costs. I booked a new round trip ticket between Oslo and Longyearbyen using frequent-flier miles, so it was free. I confirmed I could change my ticket to Bangkok for no fee. All in all, it was achievable without spending a huge amount of money, assuming everything now went according to plan.

It did not, but not the way I expected. Monday morning I went out for a 10-kilometer run. The day was beautiful and I wanted to run along the water until I reached the polar bear zone, then head back. It was a great day for photos and the temperature was not too bad, just a little below freezing. On the way back I saw one of the other runners and he asked, "Did you hear?" Apparently, the Russians had been able to fix one of the original runways, and we were now planning to go the next day instead of the next week. I kept running back to my hotel, reviewing the changes I had already made and the new changes I now needed to make.

I had made sure my new hotel rooms could be cancelled, so I was okay there. My new flight was paid for with miles and could be cancelled for no penalty. I had changed my flight to Bangkok but I could change it back with no fee. I would need to change my return flight to Oslo, which would cost something – assuming I could get a seat – but I would also cancel one night of my Oslo hotel, which would save me something. Overall, this might end up costing the same as when I started out, and without having wasted most of the backup nights I had booked in Longyearbyen. Amazingly, this could actually all work out.

~

I am one of those folks who will not truly believe something will happen until it actually does. Storing our non-polar gear, riding the bus to the airport, even getting aboard the plane, were all steps that could be reversed at any point. It was going to take boots on the ice before I was confident this was really happening.

Boots on the ice is what I got. Half of us boarded our AN-74 Short Takeoff and Landing (STOL) aircraft at Longyearbyen, with its broken seats and lack of windows, and headed north a little more than two hours. The plane would return to Longyearbyen to pick up the rest of the group, and we would run the marathon shortly after they arrived. Our landing was not as dramatic as the one in Antarctica had been, probably because it was so short. We turned around and taxied back to the camp, the door popped open, and we stepped out to the North Pole.

The actual geographic North Pole was about 30 miles away, and always moving; we would visit there later in one of the bright orange MI-8 helicopters parked nearby. First, we needed to stash our gear in one of the tents and get a short briefing from the camp director. It was quickly obvious that this was a pretty basic operation, especially when we saw the open-air barrels over holes in the ice that served as our toilet facilities.

I was scheduled for the second chopper to the Pole, which would go in about 3 hours. Since I had some time, since it was midnight at this point, and since I would be running a marathon in about 9 hours after the second planeload of runners arrived, I decided to spend my first few hours in this exotic locale taking a nap.

Once it was my turn to go, it took us about 45 minutes to get to the North Pole, with the pilots watching the GPS carefully to see where the exact geographic North Pole was. Since the ice is constantly moving, any place we landed would only be over the actual North Pole for about 10 minutes. Once the GPS showed 90.00 degrees North, we set it down and stepped out onto the top of the world.

To say that the North Pole looks like any other snowy plain would be like saying the Mona Lisa looks like any other painting. At first glance you might not realize what is so special, but as you pause and take in the meaning you can quickly get overwhelmed. At this point, I was standing where very, very few people had ever stood. Every direction was south. I could walk around the Earth by taking just a few steps and crossing every longitude line in the process. Whenever I hear someone say they are feeling "on top of the world," I will always know that I really understand what that feels like. I had made it.

I didn't make it for long, though. We had brought a bright red pole with us, which we stuck in the ice, and had a collection of city names and distances that we attached. It was picture time, and we wanted to hurry, not only because the ice was moving away from the actual Pole, but also because a storm was moving in. The skies turned grey very quickly and we started getting snow. We had only been on the ground about 10 minutes before the crew chief yelled "Two minutes!," and we all tried to take in whatever we could before the chopper took off without us.

The ride back was bumpy, but I was too busy thinking about where we had just been to pay it much notice. Also, I still had a marathon to run in a few hours, and I needed to be thinking about that. I figured I could still get a couple more hours of sleep, then eat some breakfast, and finish what I came here to do. Visiting the North Pole was amazing, but ultimately I still had the North Pole Marathon to conquer.

Then our world cracked open.

~

After sleeping for a couple hours I awoke to find the other guys in my 14-man tent were moving around, getting ready and about to get some breakfast. Knowing the other runners should be landing soon, I figured I might as well start dressing in race gear. That proved to be unnecessary.

One of the runners opened the door and yelled into the tent, "Guys, there's a big crack out here!" My definition of "a crack" changed forever as soon as I saw it. About 20 feet outside of our tent, the crack was wider than I would feel comfortable jumping, and about 3 feet deep, at which point we saw the Arctic Ocean. Looking to the right, it seemed to stretch on forever, bisecting the path near the marathon's Finish Line. Looking to the left, it cut directly across the runway. Of course.

We learned later that the second plane had been 15 minutes out when the crack appeared and they were told to turn back. If it had happened after they landed, the plane would have been stuck there at least until the runway could be repaired, assuming the two pieces of separated ice could be molded back into one. I shudder to think what could have happened if the crack had occurred during the landing itself.

The initial report from the Russian team was not too bad. They estimated they could extend the other end of the runway and be ready for flights within a day. This was a problem, but it was a problem they had already faced twice in the past week, and they were confident they could deal with it.

My own confidence was not as high, and it really hit home late that night. They had not seemed to make much progress during the day, and as I lay in my sleeping bag, it occurred to me that there was one way out of here, and it kept breaking. So far, they were 0-for-3 in runways, and it's not like the ice was getting any thicker with each passing day. The camp is only open for a month, because after that the temperatures get to the point where the ice is not thick enough to hold the plane safely. "What if," the little voice in my head kept asking, "they cannot build a runway?"

By the next day the plan had shifted to repairing the first runway, which had had time to freeze over. I made a quick satellite call to Ethan, asking him to call the airlines and make the backup travel plans I had arranged with him in advance. The only problem occurred with Thai Airways, where the ticket agent seemed to think that my Vietnamese friend did not sound like a "William Thomas," and refused to make changes until Ethan forwarded them my earlier email explaining where I would be and what I needed him to do if things went bad. It all worked out in the end.

One concern was not just the current delay, but also the possibility that any new runway could also crack and leave us here longer. We had two runners who decided they would not stick around to see what would happen, but instead, would go back on the plane that brought the second group. Both decided to maximize their experience by getting out and running, one going the full marathon distance along the runway, the other running 10K. As the latter runner put it, "My goal was to run at the North Pole. I did it. Goal accomplished." Everybody needs to decide what works best for them and their family, and this was the right choice for these folks.

The one advantage of all of this? For the rest of my life, I can begin stories by saying, "This reminds me of the time I was stranded at the North Pole..." Though as Linh has requested, "for the sake of our friendship, please don't."

~

Finally, it was race day. Two and a half days after the crack appeared, the Russian team had repaired the original runway a couple kilometers away, and it was ready for operation. Once the other runners arrived, we applauded as they were pulled into the camp on sleds behind snowmobiles. We knew they would need some time to get settled and find their gear, so there was no real rush to suit up. Before too long, though, we were all getting into our running gear, and putting our stash of drinks, gels and food in the mess tent so we could duck in for a pit stop. I also laid out a second and third set of layers on my cot in my tent so I could change out of wet clothes if I thought I needed to. This time, I remembered the underwear.

Before the race began, we had a memorial service at the Starting Line. Mike King had been the photographer for many of the North Pole and Antarctic races, and I had been looking forward to seeing him again. Sadly, in 2015, Mike had passed away suddenly, and there were a lot of us at the Pole who knew him from previous races. All of us who knew him gathered at the Starting Line to take a photo for his family, each of us holding a large photo of Mike. It was fitting, I thought, that someone who had taken such amazing photos of all of us should finally be in a photo himself.

As we prepared to go out our videographer, Dave Painter, was doing some interviews and asked me what my goal was. All I wanted to do (besides finish, of course) was beat my Antarctica time. While I had heard stories about how bad the weather at the North Pole could be, we seemed to have a mild day – about -25 to -30 degrees Celsius, which was -13 to -22 degrees Fahrenheit, and very little wind – and since these conditions were similar to what we had seen in Antarctica, I thought that was a reasonable goal. I had not seen the course yet, though, so I did not realize just how unreasonable my objective might be.

The course was a mix of two loops. The first, about 4 kilometers long, ran along the ice runway that had been broken by the crack, then followed a path toward the helicopter operations site. This gave us a few hundred meters on a smooth, paved space, and then a few kilometers along a path that had been run over multiple times by snowmobiles. Some of that trail was fairly well packed, though there were definitely spots where everything turned to mush. A lot of the route was shoe-deep, though at points it was shin-deep. It was an out-and-back loop, so we kept passing other runners in both directions. We would run eight laps along this loop for a total of 32 kilometers.

That first part was tiring, but manageable. I ran the first lap in a little over half an hour, running carefully so I could see what I was up against and could plan out the next laps. I found the areas where the snow was soft and I could expect to sink in, and figured out where it was fairly solid and I could pick up the pace and stretch out my stride.

Every lap was not the same, of course. For one thing, we were running on moving ice floes, so the ice underneath us was both contracting and fracturing, not to the point of opening up and dumping us into the Arctic Ocean, but certainly changing the underlying structure of the "ground" we were running on. One unique aspect of the North Pole Marathon is that it is run entirely on water; there is no land at the North Pole, only ice on top of the Arctic Ocean. This led to a running surface that might not be the same as it was when you last ran over it. Shifting shadows as the sun alternated going behind and back out of clouds also affected our ability to see the contrast on the ground and judge where we should step.

I realized at one point that, whereas in most marathons I would be thinking about how to tackle the miles in front of me or where the next water station was, here I was really only thinking about three or four steps ahead. I was looking down so much that I occasionally drifted away from the little flags marking the trail and started wandering off, which added distance and did not do me any good.

Theoretically, we also had to be careful of polar bears, but I was not too worried about that. While they were native to the area, the noise of the camp generally scared them away from the immediate surroundings. In case any of them came back and got aggressive, our photographers and other guards were all armed with rifles. News stories after the race always made a big deal out of this, and many online commenters seemed outraged that we were coming into the bears' territory and then preparing to shoot them, but so far they have not had a problem with polar bears at the race. In any case, my feeling was that I did not have to run faster than the polar bear, I simply had to run faster than at least one other runner.

My plan was to duck into the mess tent for drinks and gels every two laps, then consider changing my wicking layers after the 6th lap if they were really wet. That first pit stop felt so good, but I tried to make it short. I got some help with my goggles, which had iced up after only the first lap; got some liquids; then, headed back out. I had forgotten that when I stopped even for a few minutes, my body would stop generating heat; the first few hundred meters I was very, very cold as the wet clothes stuck to my body. But I soon warmed up and realized I would just have to deal with that each time I stopped.

After six laps I was very happy with my pace. I was on track to beat my Antarctica time very dramatically, perhaps even by two hours. I took the opportunity to step into my tent to change my socks, which were getting pretty wet, and since I was there I changed some of my layers too. I was wearing the same clothes I had worn in Antarctica, and since I had little need for them in Southeast Asia, it was nice to get one more use out of them. It took a little longer to get changed than I wanted, but I figured I had time since I was running so well. Sadly, that was about to come to a screeching halt.

I got back out to do the last two laps and, though I had slowed a little since the beginning, I was still doing very well. I got excited as I ran through the final lap of this first loop, and I took the opportunity to look over toward the second loop to see how people were doing. We would run this 2.5 kilometer loop four times, and I was surprised by how many people seemed to be walking. That initial surprise was nothing compared to what I was about to feel.

My first steps out of the camp and onto the second loop went fine, but within a hundred meters I was stepping through knee-deep snow, and all sense of running stopped. This was why I had seen so many walkers. The trail left by previous runners was narrow with an uneven surface. There were occasional patches of packed snow followed by deep footprints that went down to the ice. Rather than looking 3 or 4 steps ahead, I was merely trying to find the next place to put my foot.

After slogging through this for a few hundred meters, my GPS watch informed me that my pace was about 16 minutes per kilometer, more than twice what it had been earlier. So much for beating my Antarctica time. Rather than letting myself get too upset about it, I realized that this stretch was what makes the North Pole Marathon so special. This is not like running though a city, with well-marked streets cleared of obstacles and volunteers handing us water and cheering us on; this was THE NORTH POLE, and there are reasons why so few people do this. I realized the only person who was going to cheer me on was me, so I better get to it.

Richard had talked to us about being observant of the trail as well as monitoring ourselves. His point was "you need to take control of your race." That was absolutely true, and it reminded me of Ethan's advice to "run your own race" all those years ago in my very first marathon. So, on the second lap, I started shifting away from running through the footsteps of earlier runners, and instead ran a bit off to the side and made my own footprints. Rather than trying to stay on my feet while running on someone else's path, I would make my own path. It was not perfect, but I was not sinking any more than I was before, and I felt more in control of my performance.

This second loop was incredibly beautiful. While the first loop was on a wide, flat plain, this one was surrounded by pressure ridges and large pieces of blue ice, signs that various ice floes had crashed together. You could hear the sounds as the ice was coming together and cracking up, and in fact around one area I saw what seemed to be a large crack forming. I hoped it would not stretch to the camp because we just did not need any more of that hassle. I wished I could have taken some photos, but I just wanted to be finished.

After two laps I popped into the mess tent and sat for a few minutes. Plenty of runners were already done and a couple came to check on me, but I was fine. I was just trying to figure out the best way to tackle the last 5 kilometers.

Forcing myself back outside I passed one other runner on his final lap, and I just kept moving. My biggest concern at this point was falling and spraining or breaking something. If anyone got hurt, the only way out was to finish the loop or send another runner for help, which would take a while, plus of course there were not that many other runners left. As I approached the end of the third lap my mind was consumed with thoughts of water, and I decided to go into the mess tent one last time. By this time my facemask was pretty frozen and my goggles were iced over, but I was keeping them up on my head just because I could not think of a good reason to take them off.

I got to the final lap, and I was running as much as I could, trying to finish strong. I kept looking around, trying to capture the scene in my head, because I knew the chances of me ever coming back are pretty small. This place was pretty amazing. If the moon was white with a blue sky, it would look like this.

Coming through the last stretch, I ran past the targets that the Russians had been using for rifle practice, and I could see my path to the Finish Line. This area was a little easier to run on, the snow was a little harder, so I picked up the pace and kicked it into high gear, or at least as high as I could. I crossed the Finish Line, and, in that moment, all the years of planning, training, and running came to end.

I had completed the Marathon Grand Slam.

~ 11 ~
No Finish Line in Sight

Having waited 42 years before finally crossing the Starting Line of my running adventure, I am not quite ready to cross the Finish Line yet. When I first started down the Grand Slam path and told people I planned to finish it within a few years, one question I got was, "That seems so fast; what will you have left after that?" I always thought that was a silly question. Obviously, after finishing this goal, I would find another one.

A documentary I saw recently featured a subject who said, "I have had many adventures, but no achievements." That really resonated with me, because I realized that in addition to the adventure, I like knowing I have accomplished something specific. Rather than doing something just because it is fun and exciting in the moment, I would rather be doing something fun and exciting that let's me point back to it later and say, "I did that."

During the last few years of this journey I have come to realize that my life becomes much more interesting, and I feel much more comfortable, when I have a clear goal in front of me. Sometimes it is an academic goal: rather than just learning, I aim to complete a PhD. At other times, it might be a professional goal: instead of just looking for a new job, I look for a job that takes me to Singapore.

My best goals, though, the goals that by far offer me the most fulfillment, seem to be the personal ones. While my professional life is certainly important, and I want to do well and be successful, it does not define me in the way my personal goals do. The greatest pleasure I get comes from doing something I did not think I could do, and these days, that mostly means running.

So, with that in mind, here are some options that I have been thinking about to push that Finish Line farther and farther away.

Running the Abbott World Marathon Majors

I had a great time running the 2010 New York City Marathon, an experience that still stands out in my mind as one of my best. A few years later, while awaiting the results of the 2014 Tokyo Marathon lottery, I decided that finishing the Majors would be my next goal. I could see the end of the Grand Slam in sight within a couple years, and decided that if I needed another multi-year goal, then perhaps running the six biggest marathons in the world would be a good one.

Once the Tokyo Marathon was done I laid out a plan for the rest of the Majors. One of the biggest difficulties in pursuing this goal was that I could not just pay an entry fee and go. Five of the races have a lottery for entry and the biggest, the Boston Marathon, requires a qualifying time. Another option in all of these is to run on behalf of a charity and raise money, as I had done in New York. As an Ambassador for the Majors I thought I might get preferred entry, but that was not to be. I would have to compete for it or raise money, just like everyone else.

The next one on my list after Tokyo was the 2015 BMW Berlin Marathon, and the day I returned to Punta Arenas from Antarctica I got an email telling me I was in. In a similar fashion, when I got back to Norway from the North Pole I learned I had gotten into the 2016 Bank of America Chicago Marathon. The great thing about that race was that Ethan had gotten in as well, so for the first time in three years we would have a chance to run together.

As things stand now, I still have the Virgin Money London Marathon and the Boston Marathon to go. My plan is to run London in 2017 and Boston in 2018, bringing me to the end of that particular goal. As I write this, I am still waiting to hear if I make it into the 2017 London race through the lottery. If I don't, then I need to decide whether to wait and try again the following year, or instead sign up to run for a charity. The only problem with that is, I know that the only way I will run Boston is as a charity runner, and I am not sure I want to reach out to people for money in 2017 and then again in 2018.

I have talked with some runners who say the only way they want to run the Boston Marathon is by qualifying for it, and I can certainly respect that. Having said that, though, I am comfortable with my plan to run as a charity runner. While I would still like to pursue the magical "BQ" someday, I also have to strike a balance between my running and the rest of my life. Having realized that I simply do not train as hard in Asia, and not being sure how to fix that while doing everything else I am doing, I need to set realistic goals. Running as a charity runner fits that description; attaining a qualifying time, for now, does not.

Incidentally, the folks at the Abbott World Marathon Majors have also recognized the significance of this achievement, and in 2016 began awarding the 6-Star Finisher medal to those runners who complete all of the Majors. It will be a good feeling to be part of this group, though I know I still have some time before that happens. That's okay, since finishing it means I'll simply need to come up with a new goal, something I am already thinking about.

Running a Sub-4 Marathon

Many of my friends will look at this and think it sounds like an easy goal, because they have been running sub-4 for a long time. For some of them, sub-3 is the goal. As I have long realized, though, I need to set my targets based on what is important to me, not to others. I need to run my own race.

I should probably have run sub-4 years ago, but I really feel that my decision to live in Southeast Asia has led me to run more slowly. The potential seems to still be there, especially after seeing my performance in two races over the last couple of years, so I think I can do it. The question is, will I need to move back to the US to make it happen, or can I find a way to train harder in the climate of Southeast Asia? Once again, my decisions about where to live are tied to my running goals.

One thing I should consider is whether or not to work with a coach. It seems odd that, as a runner, I have worked with trainers at the gym but have never had someone train me as a runner. While there are online coaching programs that offer one option – my friends Larry and Jerico actually operate such a company, called Sweat Tracker – I think I may need to consider getting an in-person coach, since I have always found that kind of face-to-face accountability to be useful. Remember, as I said at the very beginning, I'm lazy.

Running Antarctica or the North Pole Again

Without a doubt, my trips to Antarctica and the North Pole were the highlights of the Grand Slam experience. All the other races were fun, but they were ultimately leading up to these two. The idea of being someplace where so few humans have ever been, looking around and feeling like you are in a Discovery Channel documentary, is just amazing, and try as I might, it is hard to convey to others the feelings I had when I was there. I have a link to people I met there that I do not have to people I met in Paris, Rio, or other cities. Since these were such profound experiences in my life, one question I often get is, "Would you go back?" The answer, perhaps surprisingly, is that I probably would not.

Why not? Why wouldn't I want to experience such great adventures again? Probably because they would not actually be the same great adventures the second time. Part of what made those experiences so special was thinking that this was a one-time thing. Going back a second time would involve some familiarity, and while it would still be a very cool adventure – or, more accurately, a very cold one – it would probably not be the same kind of special adventure that the original trip was, and might even take away some of the magic of that first time. So, my guess is, I probably would not go back.

Of course, one thing the Grand Slam taught me was to never say never. Before 2010 I never would have thought I would ever go to either Antarctica or the North Pole, and yet there I was. I imagine if Richard Donovan ever called me and said "I really need your help with one of these races," I would probably drop everything and go. But will I go looking for the opportunity, either to race again or visit for some other reason? Probably not.

Completing a Triathlon

So many runners I know seem to be doing triathlons. Some still run marathons while alternating with triathlons. Others have made a transition and now exclusively bike, swim, and run as a combo, though of course, if they are doing an Ironman, they still get a full marathon as part of the mix.

The idea of completing a triathlon is appealing. First of all, there's the "hey, look at the old guy!" factor, which is not a bad thing. It is nice to be able to take on something challenging and hang in there with the younger athletes. Also, it would involve overcoming a significant challenge, and that is always exciting. At least when I started running, I knew how to put one foot in front of the other; biking and swimming are another matter entirely. I have been on a bike one time in the last 30 years, and when I get into the pool I am more likely to be paddling rather than really swimming.

That latter point is one of the downsides, too. There would be a significant time commitment involved in getting ready for my first triathlon. There would also be a financial commitment, as I would obviously need a bike, and would probably need to take some weekend trips to other places for training, since Bangkok does not have much in the way of clean, open water. There would be a lot involved in aiming for this goal, but I have been so impressed by my friends who do it that I wonder if the payoff just might be worth it. It is something I will keep on the list of options, that's for sure.

Ultramarathons and Adventure Racing

When the question of ultramarathons has come up, my response has already been that "a 42.195-kilometer marathon is enough; even 42.196 is too far." Some of the more common ultramarathons around Asia tend to be 50-kilometer and 100-kilometer distances. I have had folks from South Africa invite me to come run the Comrades, the world's largest and oldest ultramarathon, a race between two cities that alternates its direction each year, resulting in an 87-kilometer race one year and an 89-kilometer race the next. Having seen friends finish these long races, in places ranging from Antarctica to Vietnam, I have certainly been inspired to try. The question is, have I been inspired enough to actually do it?

Then there are the adventure marathons, such as the Volcano Marathon in Chile and the Everest Base Camp Marathon in Nepal. There are the adventure ultramarathons, like the Marathon des Sables, a 6-day race across the Sahara Desert covering 254 kilometers. There is also the World Marathon Challenge, "The 7-7-7," which consists of 7 marathons on 7 continents in 7 days. I have friends who have done all of these, and the experiences do sound amazing.

As I think about these types of races, I feel I am more excited when I hear about other people's experiences than I am when I am actually running. Seeing a friend's photos from the Everest Base Camp Marathon or following along with the World Marathon Challenge on Facebook, it is easy to imagine myself doing them. When I am actually running, though, it may be a different story. As I was trying to get through knee-deep snow during the final five kilometers at the North Pole, I distinctly remember thinking, "This may be it for my adventure races." Having run in both Antarctica and at the North Pole, I have definitely gotten a taste of adventure racing, but I need to think carefully about whether to aim for that or an ultramarathon, or maybe just pursue some nice road races in cities I want to visit.

A Marathon in All 50 States, or a Marathon Every Month

There are some options that would lead me to run more races each year than I currently do. Since I have gotten into the habit of checking destinations off a list, I might just continue doing that. One of the instructors at my mom's gym is running a marathon in all 50 states in the

US, something that is obviously going to take a few years unless she intends to do one every weekend. In my case, I could see that taking quite a long time, since I have only run in four states so far – of my 23 marathons to date, only five have been in the United States and two of those were in Virginia – and I have a long way to go. If I want to set a goal that will carry me through a decade, this would be a pretty good one. Of course, I also need to move back to the United States for this to be realistic.

One of my North Pole colleagues is running a marathon every month, and that also sounds like a pretty fun plan. She lives in Australia, and while some of her races are around the country, most are overseas. The month before the North Pole she was in Israel, and the month after she ran the Prague Marathon. Later in the summer she took on the Moscow Marathon before heading to Chicago where I and some of our fellow Grand Slam finishers were running. I wondered how you train for something like that, and she said she does not really train in the conventional sense of recovering, building up, and tapering off. Instead, she is just always running, and each marathon is essentially a training run for the next one. This sounds like a lot of fun, and something I could potentially do while operating my own business, since I have a certain degree of flexibility with that. Of course, it also needs to be a very profitable business if I am going to fly all over the world more often than I do now.

Aiming for Shorter Distances

At some point there will come a day when running a full marathon is not the right thing for me. Either my body will say "Enough!," or I just will not take the joy in it that I do now. Rather than stopping running, I would prefer to keep doing shorter distances. Maybe I should start doing that now.

Having run three half-marathons in the last couple of years, I have gone from treating those simply as "training runs with a medal" and instead started looking at them as fun races in their own right. The half-marathon distance can be very enjoyable, since in full marathons I normally "hit the wall" beyond the half-marathon distance, and in these shorter races I can avoid that and keep a stronger, more exciting, pace going throughout the course. I also do not need a month to recover, and chances are I will not spend the next two days walking funny.

5K and 10K races can also be a lot of fun, and again, you can avoid the long recovery time and do these every week if you want to. In Singapore, for example, there seems to be at a 5K or 10K event practically every weekend, so if you do not mind paying the entrance fees – which are a lot less than you would pay for a full marathon – you could just keep doing these. For someone like me, coming from a longer distance, I may have the opportunity to actually be competitive in a shorter race, as I have built up the stamina to go far, but now perhaps can burn through it all in a short course. It is something I need to start doing, not just to train for longer races but also to have some fun now between the big events while also setting the stage for what comes later in life.

Where to Live, What to Do

As I realized over the years, any plans I have about running will be seriously impacted by decisions about where I am going to live and what work I am going to do. Living in Southeast Asia has made it easier to hop down to Australia for a marathon, but jetting off to Berlin and Chicago is more expensive than if I lived in the US. Working for a company offered me more financial resources but less flexibility than working on my own.

Throughout my military career I would change assignments and locations every few years, and I am finding my civilian life follows roughly the same pattern. So, how will my professional life and living situation continue to evolve?

Well, that's a puzzler. When I made the decision to pursue the Grand Slam I was living in Washington DC, marking time until my promotion to colonel would be finalized. When I completed the Grand Slam, I was living in Bangkok, running my own leadership consultancy, having been both a professor at Georgetown and a consultant in Singapore in the interim. I never could have imagined that path, and the point I am at now is something I never predicted, so what makes me think I know what the next 20 years, or even the next 5, will hold for me?

As much as I enjoy working for myself, I am not sure the rest of my professional life will be spent that way. There is certainly a lot to be said for it: you avoid interoffice politics, you get to set the vision and direction for your firm, you know that your skills will be the determining factor in your success or failure, you can have the occasional polar adventure, and the morning commute from home to office may only take about two seconds. Even though I am only in my second full year, the company is already profitable, and though the profits may not be huge, that definitely represents progress.

There are also downsides. I miss the interaction that comes from being surrounded by smart, thoughtful, committed people. You learn a lot when you work with the right team, and you can draw upon the energy of the group to keep yourself moving forward. One of the things I have done is occasionally work in a co-working space, with other small firms and recent startups, just to interact with people. I am not sure that is enough. I feel like I either need to add people to my company, or step into a full-time role every few years just to recharge myself.

Another aspect I need to consider is how much of an effect I hope to have. Working on my own I can add something to a firm's environment, and hopefully to their bottom line. Working for a larger organization, I have the potential to affect a multinational company, or an entire city or nation. I see some former colleagues working for large consulting firms that are helping to change the capabilities of global companies. I have many friends working for international development organizations who are making life better for people in mountain villages by ensuring they have water, or providing governments the tools to help their people start their own businesses. If I want to have a big effect like that, I either need to have such organizations as my clients, subcontract with them to help them do the work they do directly, or just go all in and work for them full time as an employee. A lot depends on what I want to accomplish beyond my own personal goals.

Much of that will be shaped by where I decide I am going to live. The decision to move overseas was a good one; in spite of the fact that I grew up as an Air Force brat, we never lived outside the country, so I am happy I made that move. Initially I was thinking I would only go to Singapore for three years or so, and then go back to the US, but that obviously changed when I decided to start up a new business and then relocated to Bangkok. Though I moved around a lot when I lived in the United States, there is something especially rewarding about landing in a new country and trying to build a life. After nearly two years in Thailand I am starting to get that urge to move again, but "Where to?" is a challenging question.

Living overseas in an age of social media is intriguing, because when you stay connected to friends back home through Facebook and Instagram, you have a good idea what life would be like if you had stayed there, and it is easy to make comparisons. When my friends post pictures from dinner at a Japanese restaurant back home, I look at those photos while I am heading out to watch sumo wrestling in Kyoto. As running friends debate going for Vietnamese *pho* in the Washington DC suburbs after a race, I am deciding whether or not I should run a marathon in Da Nang.

There are new experiences and new challenges, and in a place like Asia it is also easy to get a taste of another culture with just a quick weekend trip. As much as I enjoy living in the US, and while I know that I will be living there again at some point, I am just not sure I am ready to be done with the adventure of living overseas. The question I still need to resolve is where, exactly, I should be doing that.

~

When I made the decision in 2008 to start running and commit to completing a marathon, I was stepping out of my normal, predictable patterns, and trying something new. When I made the decision in 2010 that I needed a new goal, and would go for the Marathon Grand Slam, I was setting in motion a new attitude that I hope, and expect, I will keep for the rest of my life.

There are things I enjoy doing in my life, and I will keep doing them; change for the sake of change is rarely a good idea, so there is no need to stop something I enjoy, unless it is bad for me, and none of my habits fit that category. On the other hand, life will be more exciting as long as I keep myself open to new experiences, and seek out those things that can make me a better person who enjoys life even more. As I get older I need to remember that, regardless of my age, there are still new things to try. Even though I may not like all of them, and may never do them again, there is no way to know until I do it at least once. That is what I decided about running, and look at where it has brought me.

One thing I know for sure: crossing the Finish Line is fun, so I will keep crossing as many of them as I can…and that means I will step across a lot more Starting Lines, too.

My Marathon Grand Slam

Marine Corps Marathon
www.marinemarathon.com

Standard Chartered Marathon Singapore
www.marathonsingapore.com

Schneider Electric Marathon de Paris
www.schneiderelectricparismarathon.com

Maratona do Rio
www.maratonadorio.com.br

Sanlam Cape Town Marathon
www.capetownmarathon.com

Blackmore's Sydney Marathon
www.sydneyrunningfestival.com.au

Antarctic Ice Marathon
www.icemarathon.com

North Pole Marathon
www.npmarathon.com

Follow me on Facebook:
www.facebook.com/DrWilliamThomas

Made in the USA
Middletown, DE
15 October 2016